ALMA MATER

CAMBRIDGE POET

ALMA MATER

A Profound Study of a Great University

by

C. R. BENSTEAD

With Drawings by
EDGAR NORFIELD

FREDERICK MULLER

First published in Great Britain in 1944 by Frederick Muller Limited.
Second edition 1948.
Reprinted 1985 by Frederick Muller.
Frederick Muller is an imprint of Muller, Blond & White Limited,
55/57 Great Ormond Street, London, WC1N 3HZ.

British Library Cataloguing in Publication Data

Benstead, C. R.
    Alma mater: a profound study of a great
    university.—2nd ed.
    1. University of Cambridge   2. Cambridge
    (Cambridgeshire)—Social life and customs
    I. Title
    378.426'59'0207   LF109
    ISBN 0-584-11119-3

Printed and bound in Great Britain by
Redwood Burn Limited, Trowbridge, Wiltshire

To that Society of Learning
and Hospitality to whom I owe so much –
St. Catherine's College
Cambridge

Surely it is of this place, now Cambridge, but formerly known by the name of Babylon, that the prophet spoke when he said, 'wild beasts of the desert shall dwell there, and their houses shall be full of doleful creatures, and owls shall build there, and satyrs shall dance there; their forts and towers shall be a den for ever, a joy of wild asses.'

—THOMAS GRAY, 1736.

CHAPTER ONE

THE University of Cambridge is very old and therefore very important. Its situation in the hilly part of East Anglia proves this because in early days all places of importance were built on high ground. Also East Anglia has long been famous for clever men. Whether these men were clever before the University came, or whether the University made them clever afterwards, nobody can say. But it is certain that men always go *up* to Cambridge from whatever direction they approach, just as they always go *down* when they leave—facts which by themselves dispose of the widespread belief that Cambridge is situated in flat low-lying country. Actually the town is built on four hills: Castle Hill, where there used to be a castle; Market Hill, where there still is a market; St. Andrew's Hill, which once belonged to St. Andrew; and Peas Hill.

Gross Libel on the Cam

In view of the presence of these hills, the local rivers and brooks are unexpectedly sluggish. But they do move, and the National Fire Service is not accurate when it refers to them as 'static water'. The Cam itself is really a very pleasant river, and Cambridge men like it so much that they keep the nicer part of it to themselves by calling it the Granta. The stranger who does not know this then sets

Built on Four Hills

off downstream to the 'Pike and Eel', leaving them undis-
turbed to go upstream to the 'Orchard'—the origin of
camouflage, of course.

Mediterranean Origin of the University

The word Cambridge is derived from *cam* meaning 'that
which is crooked or eccentric', and *bridge* meaning 'a card
game'. It therefore denotes a place of wild play. This is
supported by the suggestion of wild behaviour in the origin
of the University itself, because Cambridge men still refer
to the University as their Alma Mater, and *alma* means
'an Egyptian dancing girl', and *mater* 'one who marries or
mates'. But it does show how old the University is, and
how proud Cambridge men are of their origin. *Honi soit
qui mal y pense*, as they cleverly say.

The Coming of the University Resented

Before the University came, Cambridge was naturally a
very quiet place. It had Parker's peace as well as Christ's,
so that it was most suitable for anyone who wished to study
without interruption. That is why the students settled
there. But the Mayor and townsmen did not like their
coming at all, especially as the Chancellor not only said
the University was more important than the town, but
insisted that he himself was more important than the Mayor.

The University's Authority Established

As the Mayor disagreed, the Chancellor, who was very
learned and clever, easily persuaded Henry (Part III) to
support him and say the Mayor was wrong. Henry also
said the Chancellor could have a proper court of his own,
and this at once put him in a far stronger position than the
Mayor because the Mayor had only a parlour. It also meant
that the Mayor could never hold any court cards.

The Mayor Disrespectfully Treated

The students therefore became more and more over-
bearing and were often rude to the Mayor, but even when

they 'insulted and evil entreated' him and tore his gown, using 'lewd speeches to him' and putting him 'in danger of his life', the Chancellor would not punish them. 'So it hath been and so it will be,' he said, and to silence the Mayor's protests he went so far as to excommunicate him, which was a most inconsiderate thing to do to a public official who depended so much on the postal and telephone services. Moreover, he never had any of the students

Went so far as to excommunicate him

quartered, except on some landlord who did not want them. Only the wicked townsmen were hung and drawn.

Mining Operations in Cambridge

In these very early days before there were proper colleges, most students used to live in fortified hostels or 'keeps', and they often had to dig their way into them through the refuse that collected in the streets. Hence the expression 'digging in keeps'—or, as it has now become, 'keeping in digs'—to denote residence outside a college.

To be different from the Boreales or northern students who preferred to tunnel rather than dig, the Australes or southern students called themselves 'dinkum diggers'.

Lived in fortified hostels or 'keeps'

The Cambridge Accent

These hostels were known as 'ostles', and the hostellers who lived in them were often referred to as 'ostlers'—which shows that even then the damp air from the fens was inclined to make Cambridge men a little hoarse. That is why Peter chose Friar Balsham to be his agent when he decided to set up house in Cambridge.

Stable Training Introduced

Friar Balsham was himself a keen horseman, having ridden all the way to Rome to see the Pope after Henry (Part III) had refused to make him Bishop of Ely. (That was when he first called at St. Peter's.) He therefore knew how important it was that students should lead a stable sort of life. For this reason he said that the Master of his house should be paid as much as 40s. a year to ensure that he was 'a man of circumspection in both spiritual and temporal matters'. A senior scholar, too, he said, should always share a bed with a junior one 'so that the younger be stirred by the elder to learning and good manners'. But he would allow no women to enter their rooms, not even washerwomen, 'especially young ones'. That, he said, would only be making a mare's nest.

Not even washerwomen—especially young ones

Noisy Reputation of Peter's House

Peter's House, or Peterhouse as it is now called, is the oldest college in Cambridge and therefore the most important. Being so, it has naturally produced many famous men. Kelvin, who invented Kelvinside or the Glasgow accent, was a Peterhouse man. So was Tait, who discovered sugar. Then there was Maxwell whose brays were always bonny, and Routh who did so much for coaching in the days before motor travel. All these great men were mathematicians. Peterhouse, in fact, used to specialise in producing wranglers—which explains why it has the reputation of being such a noisy college.

Peter himself took the greatest interest in his new house, particularly the front gate. This he looked after so carefully that in the end he became the patron saint of college porters, and even to-day the students talk about being gated when not allowed through the porter's lodge.

Heavenly Connexion Severed

Peter was also the first of a long line of famous clergymen who showed how much they thought of Cambridge by founding colleges there—which explains why Cambridge men are now so good. At one period, indeed, angels as well as ministers of grace were known to be in residence, and there is little doubt that they would have stayed if Cromwell's men had not treated them so roughly. One of these brutal men openly boasted that in Peterhouse he 'pulled down two mightie great angells with wings', and then crossed the street

Two mightie great angells with wings

to Pembroke where he 'broke ten cherubims'—treatment no angel or cherub could possibly tolerate. So they went away, and since then Cambridge has been quite human. *Non angeli sed Angli*, as the students cleverly put it.

CHAPTER TWO

As soon as the University authorities had settled in Cambridge, they built or hired their schools and drew up a syllabus for the students. This said the students were to study Latin, Logic and Rhetoric, and if at the end of three years they could argue properly in Latin, they could call themselves Bachelors of Arts. Then, for another four years, they could learn Arithmetic, Geometry, Music and Astronomy, and become Masters of Arts. Everything, the University said, was to be done by degrees. That is why things change so slowly at Cambridge.

The Significance of Academic Honours

The B.A. degree is just as old as the University, of course, and the letters themselves come from *baccalarius* meaning 'a cowherd' and *artium* meaning 'ability'. It therefore signifies that the holder is proficient in dairy work, and thereby not only reveals the nature of the University's earliest curriculum but explains the frequent references to Cambridge intellect as the cream of its kind.

Proficient in dairy work

M.A. comes from *magister* meaning 'a master' and *artium*, and indicates that the holder has scored a bull.

All other degrees are really fakes and, being so, are known as doctorates, from *doctor* meaning 'to adulterate or falsify'. They are therefore not worth having. That is why the University gives them away as honorary degrees.

Unpopularity of Grammarians

In addition to Masters of ordinary Arts there were also Masters of Grammar or Whichcraft, from *gramary* meaning 'enchantment or magic'. These were very clever indeed, having an absolute knowledge of ablatives as well as *verbs sap*, and they were thus far more important than ordinary M.A.s. For the same reason the Glomerels or students of 'grammarye' were more important than ordinary students, and after a while the rest of the University became so jealous that the Chancellor would not allow the Bedell in Glomery to carry the Glomery nutmeg in front of him. Nor would he let the Glomerels attend the funerals of Masters of Arts who lived in Regent Street, but the Glomerels did not really mind this because they knew that even regent M.A.s were supine in the defunctive mood. It was, in fact, the Glomerels' superior knowledge of the proper parts of speech which annoyed the ordinary students so much, the ordinary students having only improper speech, especially when referring to the Glomerels whom they quite shamelessly called 'grammaticasters'.

Principles of Child Education Appreciated

All Glomerels became masters in 'gramerscoles', and when they took their degrees, one of the things they had to do was to show that they knew the right way to teach. The regulations were most definite about this. 'The Bedyll in Arte,' they said, 'shall bring the Master of Gramer to the Vicechauncelar, delivering him a Palmer wyth a Rodde, whych the Vicechauncelar shall gyve to the seyde Master in Gramer and so create hym Master. Then shall the Bedyll purvay for evry Master in Gramer a shrewde Boy, whom the Master in Gramer shall bete openlye in the Scolys, and the Master in Gramer shall gyve the Boy a grote for hys

Ars pueros educandi difficilis est

labour, and another grote to hym that provydeth the Rodde and Palmer.'

This ceremony is clearly of great historic importance because it leaves no doubt that the principles of child education were thoroughly understood even in those days. As the Glomerels said, *ars pueros educandi difficilis est*.

University Stud Farm Started

Soon after Peter had set up house in Cambridge, the University authorities became very worried because they hadn't a proper farm where they could keep the examination cows in milk. So they consulted Pope John (Part XXII) who was a clever cattle-breeder, and he kindly gave them a Bull from the papal stud, saying that they could now be a *Studium Generale* themselves and go in for pedigree breeding.

To distinguish it from Ferdinand or the Innocent Bull which Pope Innocent (Part IV) had recently given to Oxford

Milking the examination cow

for the same purpose, the Cambridge one is always known as John Bull—which explains why Cambridge stock is so much more virile and typically British than Oxford.

The Manly Appearance of Cambridge Men

The University authorities were naturally quick to note that this would be so, and they at once took steps to avoid unnecessary delay. No student, they said, should go into a coffee house with hair shorter than a foot, and this was no passing Whim. It stands to-day, as anyone can see. Then they spoke sharply to a B.A. of Corpus for going to the 'Black Bear' with 'deformed long locks of unseemly sight and great breeches undecent for a graduate of orderly carriage'. He had, they said, made a bloomer. That is why Oxford has been allowed to wear 'bags'.

Michael Copies Peter

Once they saw how successful Peter was with his house, and particularly how important he became as the result, other good people said they would found colleges. Michael was the first of these, and he persuaded the Reverend Mr. Stanton to act as his agent—which was very cunning indeed because Mr. Stanton was Chancellor of the Exchequer in the national government of Edward (Part II), and this meant that Michaelhouse would never be short of money. But he was not so broad-minded as Peter who, we know, was not above telling even a fib, and he disliked mathematicians because, he said, they were always arguing noisily. So he would not have any in his college. Michaelhouse, he said, should attend solely to the higher education of clergymen who, as a community, badly needed it. He therefore started off with six of them, and as this was the first time any clergymen had set out to be highly educated, the ceremony of their installation was considered such an event in University life that even the Mayor was invited.

Michaelhouse stands in the old *via impura* or Foul Lane, but it is known to-day as Trinity—which shows how it has declined in importance.

The King Sends his Children to Cambridge

At this period of history English kings always had lots of children, and Edward (Part III) had so many that he decided to send them to Cambridge where they could make up a college all to themselves—which shows not only how virile he was, but also how much he thought of a University education. So he started a special college for them in King's Childer Lane, and called it the Hall of the King's Children, and it was quite a big college. Indeed, for some time to come the rest of the University noted with envy and astonishment that it was bigger than any other.

Later on Richard (Part II) also sent his children there, but he said they were not to go into residence until they were fourteen lest the lewd speech of the older students should give them wrong ideas, and later still a large gate-tower was added especially to keep out the blasts.

Great Strain Thrown on the King

When the Great Pestilence visited Cambridge, it killed

English kings always had lots of children

ever so many students and made no exception of the King's children of whom no less than sixteen of the forty died. But the King worked very hard. In quite a short time King's Hall was flourishing again, and there was no serious falling off in the supply of children until the Tudors came to the throne. Then, in spite of Henry's exertions (Part VIII), it became evident that King's Hall would have to close down. That is why it was merged with Michael-house and became Trinity. But it was a splendid tribute to Royal Endeavour while it lasted.

CHAPTER THREE

ALTHOUGH the University was very important in comparison with Cambridge, strangers to the town were always asking where it was. They could find the University Labs and the Library, and the University Arms, of course—that was in the A.A. book—but they could never find the University itself, and this bothered the University authorities a good deal because they liked strangers to see how important they were. At the same time, they couldn't always take a Bull about with them to prove it. So the Chancellor cleverly decided that the University should have a college of its own. Strangers could then be shown that.

Educational Importance of Bannockburn

There is no doubt that University Hall would have been a very fine college if it had not been burnt down almost as soon as it was founded. Unfortunately the Chancellor hadn't enough money left to rebuild it, but he knew that the Countess of Clare had a lot because her husband had just been killed at Bannockburn. He therefore asked her to rebuild it for him, and she said she would. But she also said he must call the new college Clare Hall—which meant that the University never had its own college after all, and strangers to Cambridge are still unable to find the University. It provides, too, one of the many reasons why the University authorities dislike female educationists so much.

University O.T.C. Started

On her side the Countess of Clare did not care much for the University because it was so gloomy and unsociable. That is why she said the Master of her college should preside not over a handful of dull though virtuous scholars, but over as many as nineteen Fellows or cheerful companions, from *socii* meaning 'some of the chaps'. Then, as vacancies occurred, the Fellows could choose the Master who, in turn, could help the Fellows to choose themselves, so that everybody would be in the same jolly boat or fellowship. Moreover they could be Patagonians, Tibetans, Welshmen or anybody else, as long as they were pleasant and sociable, and only six need be clergymen. But one should be a civil lawyer, and there should also be a canonist —which was a very big innovation indeed because military studies had so far been omitted from the University curricu-

Two chairs, a jug and two basins

lum. As the students said, she was obviously bent on going great guns.

Clare Dons Keenly Disappointed

When they heard what a wonderful college the Countess was going to found, all the dons eligible for appointment were naturally very excited, and therefore bitterly disappointed when she said that only those who were unmarried and poor—an unusual combination of circumstances even in those days—would be chosen. And when she cunningly arranged her endowment so that there were no more than two chairs, one jug and two basins in the whole college, they said quite openly that they had been dished.

Strange Effect of Sitting Down

Of the two chairs she provided, the Master had the one valued at a shilling, the other, valued at .1s. 4d., being reserved for famous visitors — which shows quite clearly how such expressions as 'being in the chair' and 'taking the chair' arose. From this time, indeed, the chair became a real part of University life, and the

Geological chair

possession of one revealed how important its owner was. Adam Sedgwick, who knew all about chairs, having sat in a geological one, said that 'when once a man has his rump

Privately owned

in the seat of a head, his whole moral nature becomes inverted'—which also shows that Mr. Sedgwick had never served in the Navy.

To-day the head of each faculty is always provided with an ordinary chair in addition to the bath-chair which he may privately own.

Scandalous Desecration of Great St. Mary's

Now that so many clergymen and good people were coming to Cambridge, all the churches became overcrowded

Cock crow

because the colleges had to share them with the townsmen, not having any of their own—which was a bad thing. The University owned Great St. Mary's, but the students were always going there to dispute and quarrel, and, for lack of space elsewhere, both the University luggage and the University bulls had to be kept there. So one sermon each Sunday was as much as could be preached, and that was clearly not enough. Nevertheless, this preaching of only one in a place where bulls were kept is most interesting because it undoubtedly suggested the idea of the oxometer.

Peter's Sympathetic Attitude

Fortunately both Michael and the Countess of Clare knew that even good men could not profitably spend all their time showing how good they were. That is why they said their students need not go to chapel if it interfered with their studies—which, of course, it did, especially in the early morning. But Peter saw things differently. His students, he said, should go *en masse* once a week and fire general salutes at canonical hours on other days, but they need not get up early because he knew how unpleasant it was at cock-crow.

University Authorities Exonerated

As soon as Clare was running properly, the University authorities looked round to see if there were any other wealthy ladies who might be prevailed upon to give them a college, and this time they found Marie de Valence whose husband, the Earl of Pembroke, had fortunately just been killed at a tournament on his wedding day. It is not thought, however, that the University authorities had any part in the actual arrangements of this tournament.

She wanted to call her college the Hall of Valence-Marie, but this the University authorities did not like, being apprehensive of the lewd speech of the students, and they persuaded her to call it Pembroke.

Poor Feeding at Pembroke

Like the Countess of Clare, Marie de Valence was a very determined woman. She, too, insisted that the Master and Fellows should be unmarried and poor, and she was so successful in arranging her endowment to ensure that they were, that when Uffenbach visited Cambridge seeking a background for Orpheus in the underworld, he found not only a college that was 'neither large nor fine', but also one where the cooking was definitely bad. Referring to its effect on the students, Gray said 'they are grown extremely thin'. Undoubtedly this was because she laid it down that the staff was to include only a Minor Friar instead of an experienced cook-general.

Only a Minor Friar

Local Clergymen Shocked

Although she preferred Frenchmen, Marie de Valence also said her dons could belong to any nation as long as they were pleasant sociable chaps, but she insisted on two canonists and even a medicine man—which was most disturbing to orthodox theologians, especially as she went to great trouble to provide the college with a chapel of its own.   For this reason Pembroke has always been an unconventional college.

Mellowness of Cambridge Dons

The word 'don' as applied to Fellows of the colleges at Cambridge comes from *done* meaning 'utterly exhausted'—

which shows how old they are. Many, in fact, are so old that they normally speak Latin and use English only when they have to speak to the *profanum vulgus*. At the same time, though *senes* they are by no means *seniles*. As they themselves wittily put it: *quo antiquior viola, eo dulcius carmen.*

CHAPTER FOUR

AMONG the many old-established firms in Cambridge, such as King & Harper, Flack & Judge, Rattee & Kett and Ryder & Amies, that of Gonville & Caius occupies a notably high place—on the corner of Market Hill.

Gonville & Caius Ltd.

It began in quite a small way, for Gonville started the business simply to meet the growing demand for Church requirements, but it trades to-day in a general way with

Quite good of their kind

special lines in medicine and law which are quite good of their kind. This extension of the business was brought about first by Gonville's executor, the Bishop of Norwich, and then by Dr. Caius* who put the firm on its present footing.

It was, however, the catering department which first brought the new firm before the public. As another Bishop of Norwich enviously said: 'No clerk that hath come out

Expert in ballistics or canon law

lately . . . but savoureth of the frying pan, though he speke never so holily'—which shows that Gonville allowed no Minor Friars in his kitchen.

Cambridge Theologians Offended

The local clergy and good men were not astonished when Bishop Bateman was entrusted with the task of founding Trinity Hall because, as Gonville's executor, he knew all about starting things by winding them up an his See at

---

* Readers acquainted with the Cambridge Poets will recall the well-known lines:

> A festive old Fellow of Caius
> Once took a young maid on his knaius.
> But as soon as he tried
> To embrace her she cried:
> 'You mustn't do that, if you plaius!'

Norwich had naturally given him a good insight into the Trinity's point of view. But they were when he arranged for as many as seventeen of the twenty Fellows to be lawyers because this obviously meant that the pure theologian was not regarded with favour. Moreover they considered his appointment of seven experts in ballistics or canon law to be excessive, but here they were wrong, as they had to admit when the splendid gunnery of a Trinity Hall man did so much to destroy the Spanish Armada.

Tusser's Remarkable Discovery

Lord Howard of Effingham did this, and he is only one

Invented the two-ended sofa

of the many important men who studied at Trinity Hall. There were, for example, Chesterfield who invented the two-ended sofa; Cockburn who made port to everybody's satisfaction; Lytton who spent his last days in Pompeii; and, most famous of all, Tusser who wrote down *The Five Hundred Points of a Good Husband*. Hitherto not even happily-married wives had realised their husbands had so many.

Borough Boys Outwit the University

When they saw these new colleges being built, and noticed how important everybody connected with them became, the townsmen said they would have one too, and this worried the University authorities very much because, although they wanted all the colleges they could get, they did not like dealing with the townsmen. But the townsmen

Dying faster than the town clergy could sing

cunningly went to the King, and he said they could, so the University had to agree.

The Guilds of Corpus Christi and the Blessed Virgin clubbed together to put up the money. Even so they could not raise enough for more than two Fellows in addition to the Master. The college was therefore a small one. But what annoyed the University most was the shameless way the Guilds said that the scholars should always be available to sing masses, free of charge, for the souls of guildsmen who were then dying faster than the town clergy could sing.

Unilateral Abrogation of Pact

For this reason the College of Corpus Christi and the Blessed Virgin never really liked its founders, and before long the scholars neglected even to pray for the souls of departed guildsmen—which was very ungrateful of them because the guildsmen, when alive, had not only given them ever so many candles as rent, but also a wonderful drinking horn out of which they could take wine *in piam memoriam fundatoris*. The townsmen therefore took a dim view.

The Town Goes Into Training

The Mayor was particularly upset about this, and when he presided over a meeting of tenants and interested townsmen at the Guildhall, he said that as far as could be seen without candles, they should apply a writ of *Habeas Corpus*. So they chose James of Grantchester to captain the town side and 'bound him with an oath to do whatsoever they should command him'—which shows that even in the fourteenth century the townsmen of Cambridge were politically mature.

To get some practice before playing the College, they had a friendly game with a neighbouring landowner whom they quickly defeated, taking away his ox and his ass and everything that was his. Afterwards they destroyed the house of a University bedell to obtain experience in demolition, and then, being satisfied with their training, they went round to the College.

The Town Easily Beats Corpus

At first the College refused to play them. This, they thought, was most unsporting, so they burst open the gates and 'as if the readiest way to pay their rents was to destroy their landlords, they fell violently on the Master and Fellows therein'—the origin of the college 'squash', of course. They fell, too, on the scholars, and taking no notice of the lewd speeches directed at them, deliberately broke all their chambers—which was, perhaps, carrying things unnecessarily far.

The Chancellor Angered

This easy win encouraged the townsmen so much that they decided to play the University itself, and although it was late at night and they had no appointment, they called straightaway on the Chancellor to arrange a match. But he also refused to play. He described their challenge as presumptuous, and they had to threaten him with fire and sword before he would sign a deed renouncing all the University's privileges and binding the University authorities in the huge sum of £3,000 to 'subject themselves to the power of the townsmen and free the townsmen from any actions, real or personal, which might arise from this occasion'—all of which was very improper of them although it does show how cleverly they were directing James to lead them.

The Chancellor was naturally most annoyed. *Delendus est Cantepons*, he said.

The Mayor's Memorable Speech

After leaving the Chancellor, the townsmen went to Great St. Mary's where they found all the University's most important documents. This pleased them immensely because they were the very things for starting a bonfire on Market Hill. So they started one, and everybody danced and shouted just as they do to-day. 'Be of good cheere, my masters,' the Mayor said. 'We have thys day lyghted such a fyre as shal flamme evry fyfthe of Novembr and Armystyce Nyght tyl fyrewode vanyshe from Cantebrig.' Which is very true.

Precious Evidence Destroyed

Among the townsfolk who gathered round the bonfire to rejoice was a strong-minded old lady called Margaret Sterr because she was always sterring things, and this time she not only sterred up the ashes of all the important documents but scattered them about as well. 'Away with the learning of the clerks!' she cried. 'Away with it!'

In that way the University lost all its records, and since

then it has never been able to prove that Cantaber, a Spanish prince, decided on Cambridge as the University's home many hundreds of years before Oxford was thought of—which is another reason why the University authorities dislike women so much.

The Townsmen Ruled Off-Side

As soon as the bonfire had gone out, the townsmen went

'Away with the learning of the clerks !'

to Barnwell Priory, an institution they disliked almost as much as the University, and after making a few alterations there, they took the precaution of cutting down a grove of trees that looked rather like a possible row of gallows. Indeed, at this stage of the game they were scoring freely all round the wicket, and there is no doubt that they would have won by a big margin if 'the warlike Bishop of Norwich

had not casually come to Cambridge with some forces'
and, using nutmegs, 'seasonably suppressed their madness'.

The townsmen were terribly disappointed, of course,
but they could not play the Norwich diocese as well as the
University, especially as the Chancellor unsportingly told
the King and the King said the match was not to count in
the championship. Moreover, he sternly rebuked them for

Took away their privileges

not playing the whistle, and to punish them, not only made
them return the deed which the Chancellor had signed but
took away the few privileges which the University had not
already taken because they were hardly worth having.
Later, however, he restored these—which was really kind
of him though the townsmen thought it peculiarly funny
Only the University thought it funny ha-ha.

University Fixture List Adjusted

Largely on account of the rough behaviour of the towns-men on this occasion, the University no longer plays the town side. Instead, tradition is maintained by friendly matches between the students, who take the place of the townsmen, and the University authorities assisted by the local police, who between them take the place of the students, and the rules are framed so that a good time is had by all except the owners of inflammable property near Market Hill. Nor is the Mayor forgotten. He presides at the police court next morning.

Presides at the police court next morning

CHAPTER FIVE

Now that they knew they could beat the town, the University authorities felt more important than ever, and by way of showing it, they told the Mayor and Corporation to clean the town drains.

Continental atmosphere

The Town in Bad Odour

There was, the Chancellor said, a Continental atmosphere about the place which was not at all in keeping with his idea of clean fun. In fact, not only students but even Fellows and Masters were falling sick simply through walking down Trinity Lane—which shows that the town really was aromatic, as indeed the Mayor did not attempt to deny. He was, though, very cunning about it. Knowing that the Chancellor couldn't possibly object to anything which was done by degrees, he said that for a start he would not allow the townsmen to leave their dung on Market Hill for longer than a week, and he would see that they cleaned the 'common sege' once every three years, an undertaking at which the Chancellor naturally turned up his nose. As the students cleverly said, *avis nidum paulatim purgat*.

Remarkable Feat of Sanitary Engineering

But the Mayor would not agree with the Chancellor about cleaning the King's Ditch. This was a very big ditch running up Pembroke Street and through the town—which meant that lots of people were privy to it. And when the Chancellor said the Mayor should clean it, the Mayor refused, saying that the King ought to because, after all, it was his ditch. Also Mayors were not necessarily sanitary engineers even in a democracy. The Chancellor therefore disliked the Mayor more than ever.

In the end the Chancellor went to Parliament and asked them to make the Mayor do the cleaning, but Parliament merely appointed a Royal Commission to look into the Ditch, and as they were still looking into it when a hundred years had gone by, the Chancellor and the Mayor agreed that their chances of survival would be increased if they cleaned it themselves. So they cunningly made a river with the water of nine wells and ran that through the Ditch—a most ingenious idea which Hercules himself was glad to copy.

Non Benedict sed Benedictine

In that way Cambridge, unlike Oxford, got rid of its high streets.

Distilleries Set Up in Cambridge

Although they were often poor and had no chairs to sit on, the University authorities nevertheless liked a good table, particularly a square one because that is the very foundation of a good meal.   So when the monks wanted to build a college in Cambridge, they were all for it.   *Non Benedict sed Benedictine*, as they jokingly said.   That is why Monks' College was so popular from the start, in spite of its unattractive situation on the banks of the Cam opposite the electric-power station.

Lolling about instead of working

Suggestion of Slackness Refuted

But far more important than even an assured supply of liqueur was the proposal to build God's House. Nothing like it had happened before, and the dons were exceedingly pleased for a number of reasons. Not only did it show that Cambridge was still being considered as a worthy educational centre, but it also revealed that Cambridge was more highly thought of than Oxford, and this itself was just as gratifying as it was unexpected because people had been saying that the Cambridge students were cutting their lectures and lolling about instead of working—those who were said to have done so were known as lollards, of course —and the Archbishop of Canterbury had recently come all the way to Cambridge and spent such a long time questioning the dons that they had begun to think he suspected them of lolling about too. So they were very pleased indeed at this sign of complete confidence in them which the proposal to build God's House revealed.

Caning of Schoolboys Officially Approved

When, however, Mr. Bingham, who was the local agent, said the intention was that God's students should study only grammar and become schoolmasters, they were just a little disappointed and even surprised, though the Glomerels were not because they knew that everything began with the Word and that, as the Scriptures said, the Word was God. Besides, they definitely thought the idea a good one. It not only showed that they were very important indeed, but it let everybody know that the schoolmaster's 'rodde' had the approval of the highest possible authority, and this in turn made it clear that methods of teaching which forbid its use are contrary to the wishes of that authority and therefore most improper.

God's House Unhappily Christened

Unfortunately God's House was not at all the right sort of name to give to a college at Cambridge because the students are very keen on rowing and have boat races on the

Cam, and one simply could not have crowds of students on the towpath exhorting the Deity to greater effort with the oars. It was irreverent enough having them call upon Jesus. That is why God's House was ultimately allowed to pass in normal hereditary descent and become Christ's.

Curious Method of Racing on the Cam

The students always hold their big races in June and call them the May Races to deceive unwanted strangers.

'Please may I leave the river?'

They tell their friends the actual dates privately, of course. But they cannot race at all, really, because the river is so narrow. This means that they have to use special boats which are very long and thin. These boats hold nine students and are therefore known as 'eights'.

To introduce the competitive element, they row one behind the other from Baitsbite, each boat trying to catch the one in front before it reaches the 'Pike and Eel', and as there isn't any room to pass, a boat that succeeds in overtaking another cannot avoid bumping into it. The name 'bumping races' does not therefore mean that the races themselves are necessarily rough, or that anyone is bored—except, possibly, among the spectators.

Floral Decoration for the Winner

As soon as a boat is bumped, it doesn't have to race any more that day, and its cox raises his hand, meaning: 'Please may I leave the river?' But on the following day it changes

Sidney overtakes Lady Margaret

places with the boat that bumped it, and this goes on year after year so that in course of time a boat may bump its way to the end of the line and have nobody in front of it to bump. It is then said to be Head of the River—being, of course, nearer to the source of the Cam than any other boat—and the students in it are allowed to wear roses round the brims of their straw hats. Nowadays, however, people who have not studied botany think this pansy.

Occult Practices in Rowing

Unlike Oxford, Cambridge has always known how to row properly. This is because mathematics are taken seriously at Cambridge whereas at Oxford they are not, and in rowing it is essential to be able to count accurately up to ten. No other number will do. Experience has shown that if a boat is counted to up to ten, it goes faster than it does when counted to up to nine or eleven. Therefore each boat must carry someone who is able and free to count up to ten. That is why a mathematical student is required as cox. His title, cox, derives from the fact that

Old Blues

Cambridge boats are always cocks of the fairway or proper method of rowing.

Reprehensible Behaviour on the River

Students who are unable to find boats to row in because the Cam is so narrow, remain on the towpath and give advice. All students are competent to do this. They move along with the boats—which is not difficult—and from time to time encourage them to go faster in terms such as 'Come on, Caius!' and 'Go it, Emmanuel!' If, as may happen,

Caius does so but Emmanuel does not, and a collision occurs, then they say quite frankly that Cauis caught Emmanuel by the gut, or wherever it was. Or it may be that Sidney has overtaken Lady Margaret at Grassy Corner, a very public spot, after being told to give her ten, and again they say so, with relish or otherwise according as their sympathies lie with Sidney or Lady Margaret. It is thus clear that God's House could never put a boat on the river and, that being so, there was little point in its preservation.

Obvious Patriotism of Rowing Men

Being strong and manly young men accustomed to going all out for their side, rowing men are always patriotic, and in later years when their faces have become red and their moustaches white, they often turn out in undersized schoolboy caps of faded blue to show how patriotic they really are. They are then known as Old or Genuinely True Blues.

Of Bacchanalian character

Requiem

After the final race the students relax, and if they have
made a lot of bumps, they celebrate their success with a feast
of Bacchanalian character known as a bump supper or
'bumper'. (Hence the use of this word to denote a brim-
ming glass and a satisfactory abundance of good things.)
Then they have a bonfire or 'bonner' at which they sometimes remove the memory of their suffering by burning the
boat that caused it. (The true significance of 'burning
one's boats', of course.) And they always wear highly inflammable coats which are called blazers, from *blaze* meaning
'to burst into flame', so that a bump supper is inevitably a
bright affair even if it is not a burning question.

CHAPTER SIX

IN addition to teaching themselves to row, Cambridge
students also give an exhibition of rowing on the Thames
so that Oxford can see how it is done, and every year, when
there isn't a war, they lead a procession of boats from Putney
Bridge to the Mortlake Brewery. This has come to be
known in error as the University Boat Race. But it has
also become a national event, and it is therefore reported
by B.B.C. commentators. Sometimes they are Old Blues
engaged for the occasion. The broadcast commentary is
then much more interesting than the race itself. It runs like
this:

FIRST HEARTY VOICE (*for the moment suppressed to a stage
whisper*): Is it all right for us to start now?

NORMAL VOICE (*suppressed to an exasperated whisper*):
Yes, go ahead.

FIRST HEARTY VOICE (*still suppressed*): You mean they
can hear me now?

NORMAL VOICE (*with emotion*): Yes, yes! For heaven's
sa——

FIRST HEARTY VOICE: Oh! (*Then blossoming to full
heartiness.*) Hullo, everybody! Good morning to you all

Engaged for the occasion

if you've just tuned in. Here we are in our launch at Putney Bridge. The crews will be out any moment now, but there's just time for me to tell you about the tremendous scene here Thousands of people, don't you think, Prendergast?

SECOND HEARTY VOICE: Oh yes, definitely thousands.

First H.V.: Might be a Bank Holiday, of course. Everybody's singing and shouting and wearing light-blue ribbons and rosettes. Can you see any dark blue, Prendergast?

SECOND H.V.: Only one—no, two. Cambridge are favourites, I think.

FIRST H.V.: Yes, I'd say Cambridge are favourites. Perfect rowing weather too. The snow's just left off. There's now a nice breeze from the north-east. You haven't a spare muffler, by the way, Prendergast?

SECOND H.V.: Sorry, old boy. I'm wearing both mine.

FIRST H.V.: Oh! Well—er—tremendous number of craft about. Never seen so many, have you?

SECOND H.V.: No, definitely no. But blow me down! Do you see what I see, Cholmondeley—over there, in that magenta motor boat?

First H.V.: Why, if it isn't—yes, it's Betty Grabie! And what a——

Second H.V.: That would be Oxford coming up to the stake boat now, wouldn't it?

First H.V.: By Jove, you're right! It's Oxford. They're coming out first as challengers, of course. And what a crew! Splendid lot—splendid!

Over there—in that magenta motor-boat

Second H.V.: Oh yes, definitely splendid.

First H.V.: Of course, when I stroked Cambridge in '63——

Second H.V.: Ah, I remember that well. You won by rather less than usual, didn't you?

First H.V.: Barely nine lengths. But what a race! How many do you reckon we shall win by to-day?

SECOND H.V.: Oh, fifteen to twenty, m'boy. Fifteen to twenty.

FIRST H.V.: Quite a close thing, in fact.

SECOND H.V.: Yes, pretty evenly matched, by all accounts.

FIRST H.V.: Look! There they are! Cambridge coming up now. Splendid——

SECOND H.V.: Magnificent! Look at Four's leg muscles.

FIRST H.V.: Ah, Cambridge have chosen the Surrey side, as I thought. Good strategy that, Prendergast. Get the bend, what!

SECOND H.V.: Eh? Oh, that—yes, of course. Very powerful telescope Betty's using, don't you think?

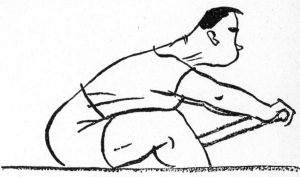

Look at Four's leg muscles

FIRST H.V.: Eyes in the boat, Prendergast, m'boy! Eyes in the boat!

SECOND H.V.: Haha! Very good, Cholmondeley. We rowing men must keep our eyes in the boat, what!

TOGETHER: Hahaha!

FIRST H.V.: Look out! They're going to start!

SECOND H.V.: Yes, they're coming forward! They're——

FIRST H.V.: No, they're going back! This excitement is really too much.

SECOND H.V.: Bow's fiddling with his seat.

FIRST H.V.: Dear me, how very awkward!

SECOND H.V.: Look! They're coming forward again! They're going to——

FIRST H.V.: Yes!

SECOND H.V.: Yes!

TOGETHER: They're off!—two—three—four—five—six——

FIRST H.V.: Forty-eight in the first half minute. Pretty good, that, by Jove! You get Oxford's, old man?

SECOND H.V.: Forty-nine at least.

FIRST H.V.: Remarkable! Colossal!

SECOND H.V.: Nothing in it at present. Barely half a canvas. Yes, half a canvas, I think, Cholmondeley. Don't you?

FIRST H.V.: Just under, I'd say. A third, perhaps, or two-fifths.

SECOND H.V.: They're settling down now.

FIRST H.V.: Oh, beautiful rhythm! The very poetry of motion! Both crews are swinging as one man—as you were, as two separate men, I mean. This is Cambridge: in–out..in–out..in–out..in–out..in–out..in–out.

SECOND H.V.: And this is Oxford: in–out..in–out..in–out..in–out..in–out.

FIRST H.V.: Just shows you, eh, Prendergast?

SECOND H.V.: Oh, yes, definitely. Cambridge much the better crew. But Oxford's leg-drive is good——

FIRST H.V.: Look! Oxford's challenging already! They're giving her ten—ten of the very best! Yes, they are—yes, they're going up! What a race! What a race!

SECOND H.V.: Square two!

FIRST H.V.: This is terrific—phenomenal! Cambridge is losing the lead!

SECOND H.V.: Impossible!

FIRST H.V.: Yes!

SECOND H.V.: No, there's still half a canvas, wouldn't you say?

FIRST H.V.: By Jove, I believe you're right! Just over, if anything. Two-thirds or, perhaps, three-fifths. But——

SECOND H.V.: Look! Cambridge have accepted! They're giving her ten!

FIRST H.V.: And what a ten! Oh, magnificent, prodigious! The Oxford stroke is looking over his shoulder to see where they've gone.

SECOND H.V.: Square three.

FIRST H.V.: This is amazing. There'll soon be water between them. Yes, that is water between them, isn't it, Prendergast?

SECOND H.V.: Looks very like it to me. They're still on the river.

FIRST H.V.: If only I could find words for this splendid, this colossal race—these two magnificent crews fighting it out between them like a—like a pair of—yes, like a pair of eight-legged white beetles crawling with such purposeful yet unhurried gait upon grey waters. It's terrific. Oxford can never stand the pace. Yes, they're getting short already.

SECOND H.V.: Oh yes, definitely short. And ragged too.

FIRST H.V.: Oh, definitely ragged. And I don't like Two's puddle. Wants more in it, don't you think?

SECOND H.V.: Definitely. Oh yes, definitely wants more in it.

FIRST H.V.: I'll give you their rate of striking. This is Cambridge: in – out ... in – out ... in – out ... in – out ... in – out ... in – out.

SECOND H.V.: And this is Oxford: in – – out .... in – – out .... in – – out .... in – – out .... in – – out.

FIRST H.V.: Astonishing how form tells, eh, Prendergast?

SECOND H.V.: Square four.

FIRST H.V.: Look!

SECOND H.V.: Where!

FIRST H.V.: Cambridge are just going to shoot Hammersmith!

SECOND H.V.: Shoot Hammersmith? Why, whatever for?

FIRST H.V.: There they go! Oh, perfect shooting!

SECOND H.V.: What, did they hit? I can't see properly at this distance.

FIRST H.V.: Now Oxford's shooting!

SECOND H.V.: Quite a barrage, what!

FIRST H.V.: By Jove, this is wonderful—astounding! Cambridge are taking Oxford's water, see?

SECOND H.V.: Really, Cholmondeley! Is that quite nice of them?

FIRST H.V.: What strategy! What watermanship!

SECOND H.V.: Seems to me they've taken the whole river. Do you think Betty would lend us her telescope?

FIRST H.V.: Heavens above! Look! Look! Oxford's bow has caught a crab! Unprecedented! Phenomenal! Did you ever know crabs to come so far up-river as this, Prendergast?

SECOND H.V.: Well, come to think of it, I've had some

Unprecedented! Phenomenal!

pretty good crab salad at Henley in my time—ones at Phyllis Court.

FIRST H.V.: Oh, very good! Very good indeed! Ones that Phyllis caught!

TOGETHER: Hahaha!

FIRST H.V.: Still, plenty of devil in 'em yet, what! Magnificent fight they're putting up. Absolutely Homeric. They're hanging on to Cambridge——

Second H.V.: That's Cambridge, isn't it, Cholmondeley —just going over the horizon now?

First H.V.: Yes, indeed, Cambridge is—by Jove, she's spurting!   They're giving her ten!

Second H.V.: What, again?

First H.V.: They must have smelt—sighted, I mean— the Brewery.

Second H.V.: Cambridge, square eight.   Oxford, square six.

First H.V.: I'll give you their rate of striking.   This is Cambridge: in–out–in–out–in–out–in–out–in–out–in–out. And this is Oxford: innn – – – ou–t . . . . . . innn – – – ou–t . . . . . . innn – – – ou–t . . . . . inn – – – out—Great Heavens! —in – – out—They're spurting!—in–out . . in–out . . inout . inout inoutinoutinoutincredible, Prendergast, incredible!

Second H.V.: What, have they smelt—er—sighted the Brewery too?

First H.V.: Must have.   By Jove, can't you?

Second H.V.: Seems pretty good to me.

First H.V.: But they can't do it now—never.   How many lengths would you say, Prendergast?   Twenty-three?

Second H.V.: And a canvas at least.   But it's difficult——

First H.V.: Look, there's the official figure going up now.

Second H.V.: Twenty-four lengths.   Just as I thought.

First H.V.: Magnificent race.

Second H.V.: Definitely.   Oh yes, definitely a magnificent race.

Must have smelt the brewery

FIRST H.V.: Cambridge are quite refreshed already, I see. Remarkable after such a gruelling struggle.

SECOND H.V.: Oxford never let up the pursuit for a moment, and their finish——

FIRST H.V.: Stupendous! Phenomenal to a degree! Nothing like it for years. Magnificent race...........

CHAPTER SEVEN

KING'S is a very large chapel opposite the K.P. café. There is a college attached to it, but that is unimportant, being until recently just a finishing school for Eton boys whose bad manners had come to the notice of Henry (Part VI) when he was at Windsor.

Magni Nominis Umbra

The University authorities were very disturbed at the idea of having this finishing school at Cambridge because

Definitely adumbrated trouble

Henry (Part VI) did not throw an ordinary shadow. He cast a holy shade, and that was far more unpleasant, as they soon discovered when he said that boys from Eton who came into residence should be 'exempt from the power, dominion, and jurisdiction of the Chancellor, Vice-Chancellor, proctors and ministers of the University' in all matters of discipline. This, they said, definitely adumbrated trouble, and when they were forced to give the King's students degrees without any examination or argument at all, they felt not so much put in the shade as totally eclipsed.

The University Authorities Certified

Henry was going to build his college at Oxford until he was told that the students there were always lolling about and talking with a funny accent, and when the University authorities at Cambridge heard this, they were more angry than ever and bitterly regretted their own good behaviour. He kept them hanging about too. It was four hundred years before the college was completed, and they did not like being detained for such a long time during His Majesty's pleasure.

Then he moved God's House bodily to another site, and the dons there were terribly upset.

The King Drops a Brick

When he saw how unpopular he was, Henry was very frightened indeed, and he would not come to Cambridge even to lay the foundation stone of his chapel. He said there was 'such a sad mortality proceeding from the infection of the air and that caused by the unclean keeping of the streets' that he would, instead, send 'thidder our Cousin the Marquess of Suffolk' who was a well-known sporting nobleman. (The origin of passing the buck, of course.) But he lost a lot of prestige by doing so. As the dons said: 'Let him that is without sin lay the first stone.' More tersely, though, the Chancellor added: *Umbra sancta, mi pes!*

The Mayor and the Chancellor Collaborate

The townsmen were annoyed because Henry started to build his chapel right across the main shopping thoroughfare through the town—which they thought inconsiderate. Also, to make room for the college grounds, he cleared away the big docks by the river and all the shops and houses between them and the road, and that, the townsmen said, was not only inconsiderate but ruinous for trade. So the Chancellor simply had to agree with the Mayor that something should be done. *Necessitas miros socios facit*, as the students wittily put it. But Henry at once surrounded his college with walls and proper fortifications, and when a task force of M.A.s launched an offensive with the support of canonists, the defenders were able to regroup and iron out any salients by blunting the attacker's spearheads before they could fan out at the key strategic points—which was most disappointing for the University. As Kipling wrote: 'The tumult and the shouting dies, but Eton and King's remain.'*

The Queen Threatens Cambridge

All this was naturally very worrying for the University authorities, and when the Queen said she wanted to found a college too, they were filled with alarm and despondency. 'Besecheth mekely Margaret quene of England your humble wif,' she said, and for that reason alone Henry could not do other than agree. But although she followed Henry's example and refused to have a Master, preferring a President as he had a Provost, she did say her college should be an

---

*Readers acquainted with the Cambridge Poets will recall the verse which, at the time, provided the words of what dance bands called a 'novelty number':

> All are from Eton, all the King's men.
> They come up to Cambridge and go down again,
> All those from Eton who are King's men.
>   Whate'er they do, their destiny
>   Is high degree, but don't you see,
>   They dwell in splendour on K.P.
>   To put a little tone into the Varsity.
> Noble sons of the Upper Ten,
> They come up to Cambridge, and go down again,
> All those from Eton who are King's men.

ordinary one. The University, however, was still very nervous. *Timeo reginas et collegia ferentes*, as the Chancellor neatly put it.

Henry Suffers a Blackout

Unfortunately for Margaret, the big Yorkshire-Lancashire match began before she could get her college started properly, and everybody was so excited and busy placing their bets

Dwelt in splendour on K.P.

that there was no money left for education. And when Yorkshire won, not only did Henry himself lose all substance and therefore the means of casting even a holy shade, but Margaret herself went back to France, and the college would undoubtedly have died from night starvation if the President had not persuaded the new Queen to take Margaret's place and act as foster mother. That is why Queen's became Queens'.

Mystery College Founded

One of the early Provosts of King's was a cheerful man called Woodlark because he was always playing jokes, and he thought it would be quite amusing to found a real college since there wasn't much fun, after all, in being head of a mere finishing school. So he built a nice ordinary college just outside and called it Catharine Hall after a lady he knew,

Could have wished her somewhat higher

and everybody tried to guess who she was. In the end they decided she was one of Edward (Part IV) 's favourites of whom it was said 'there was nothing in her body one could have changed except one would have wished her somewhat higher'. This was because Catharine Hall was very beautiful to look at but suffered, for some time, from 'lowness of endowment and littleness of receipt'.

Woodlark, who was a Boreal, was quite undecided about

what he was going to have for her crest, and when asked, could only say: 'Ah weel, now——' And it has been ever since.

Woodlark's Rude Retort

When Queens' objected because Woodlark put Catharine Hall nearly opposite their front gate, he just laughed, saying: *'Feli licet reginam spectare. Ita quid?* Which explains why Queens have never really liked Cats. Queens' said 'Scat!' of course.

Feminine Charm of Jesus Men

The attitude of the University authorities towards these colleges was one of deep reserve because anything which had to do with women was suspicious, and they were therefore very pleased indeed when the Bishop of Ely said he would found a college and at the same time get rid of some women who, he agreed, had no business in a university town except as bedmakers. There were, incidentally, only two left in the place he wanted for his college, and when they were gone it would be a real nunnery. So he turned them out, and to make sure that he would have influential support when he was called to account, he named his foundation the College of Jesus, the Blessed Virgin Mary, St. John the Evangelist and St. Rhadegund.

No other Cambridge college lives in a nunnery, and this accounts for the sweet nature and feminine charm of Jesus men to-day.

CHAPTER EIGHT

THE University authorities have always been very clever in what they do, as we have seen. This is because they are very old and therefore very wise. Exactly how wise they are can easily be seen from the gallery of the Senate House when they are assembled there. Disrespectful students say it is like looking down on a collection of ostrich eggs—

which is why so much in the University is said to be done *ab ovo*.

Choosing a Chancellor

At first the Chancellor or headmaster of the University was always one of the dons. As long as this was so, he was naturally very wise and learned. His assistant, too, the Vice-Chancellor, was also a don. The University was therefore very well run in those days. But when the King saw how important the Chancellor was, he thought it a pity that the job should be confined to the University, and as time went on all sorts of odd people were made Chancellors— even ex-Prime Ministers. This means that the Chancellor to-day is merely *caput non utile sed magnificum*, as the dons

Spice is added by the Esquire Bedells

put it, and that the real head is the Vice-Chancellor who, as Master of a college, is *utillimus*, of course, though not as a rule *magnificus*.

University Officials Compelled to Walk

In order to go anywhere officially, neither the Chancellor nor the Vice-Chancellor can take a taxi. They have to walk in procession. That is why they never call on Oxford.

This restriction also limits the choice to those people who can still walk, bath-chairs not being allowed in official processions, which are occasions of great dignity. Spice is added by the Esquire Bedells who march in front carrying the University nutmegs.

The Dons' Keen Sense of Fun

At the Senate House the Chancellor often had to make a speech. This was all right when the Chancellors were real scholars, but it was most awkward when they were not because they could not necessarily speak Latin. Nor could mathematical and scientific Vice-Chancellors always do so fluently and help them out. The University authorities therefore had to appoint someone who could, and because he never had to speak in public where Latin is not understood, they cleverly called him the Public Orator.

Whenever important people such as retired admirals and engine-drivers of Cabinet rank are given honorary degrees, the Public Orator has to tell them on behalf of the University how nicely they have steered their battleships and driven their trains, but this is quite in order because admirals and engine-drivers can always understand Latin. To an admiral of the Second World War he might say, for example:

Ave, Imperator! Risuri te salutant.

Magnum est nomen Cantepontis, sed maximus est qui in nomine Academiae loquitur. Ecce homo!

Arma Wopumque cano. Naves Wopi perdisti. Nobilem ducem Woporum expulisti. Sed lingua Wopi vivit. Gloria mundi, tuesdi resti weekque manet Wopus, et te, O ridiculus mus, oportet dicere Wop. Ars longa, vita brevis, sed rivita in dentibus haeret. Laus Wopo!

Ave, Imperator!

Oculi omnium aspiciunt et in te sperant, sed tu non das iis escas illorum tempore opportuno—non unam sausageam. Tum sol major est quam terra, tu pauper piscis, cum magister artium major est quam miser nauta—tantum plus ita, tantivy, tantivy, tumtum tumtum. Lo sputare.

Eheu! Fugaces labuntur anni. Amor vincit omnia, et omnibus donis tuis quae ex larga liberalitate tua sumpturi sumus. In vino veritas. In telephono sanitas. Si viam invenire vis, custodem civilem roga. Wopee!

Attempted Theft at the Senate House

The ceremony of giving a doctor's degree used to be most impressive. It involved a cap and a kiss, a book and a ring, and, of course, a chair. But to-day the recipient of the degree must buy them himself if he wants them.

The ring was a very old one indeed. It once belonged to Minerva, and it was engraved with her motto: *Si perdam, pereo.* ('If I say damn, I perish.') It was therefore quite valuable, and the last time it was used, the recipient liked it so much that he hung on to it, and before he would give it back the Senior Esquire Bedell had to speak sternly to him several times, saying: '*Perdamnatus sum si facis, tu periens!*'*

Kissing Banned on Scarlet Days

When they heard that women wanted to come up to

Decided to wash out kissing altogether

Cambridge and take degrees, the Masters of the colleges were terribly excited because the Vice-Chancellor would have to kiss them, and they all wanted to become Vice-Chancellors as soon as possible. But on second thoughts they realised there was not really much fun in *suavium*, 'the kiss of holy love', and a spot of genuine *osculum* was rather wasted on the type of woman that took degrees.

* 'I'm damned if you do, you perisher!'

Anyhow, it was out of place in the Senate House. So they
decided to wash out kissing altogether—which shows how
strong-minded they were.

This also meant that they wouldn't have to kiss the
admirals any more—which was a good thing.

The Dons' Keen Appreciation

Of all the ceremonies at the Senate House, the installation
of the Chancellor himself was naturally the most important.
It was also a very jolly occasion, especially when the Chancellor was a Royal Duke because Royal Dukes are always
kind and good men, and they used to give the dons nice
comfortable jobs and even make them bishops. The
University was therefore greatly in their debt. That is
why the Cambridge Poets never welcomed them with
ordinary verses but always with oweds.*

Gray said the whole University was a little tipsy on these
occasions—from the passive of *tibo, tibere, tipsi, tipsum,* of
course, meaning 'I am tipped or given a present'.

Early Importance of the Proctors

To see that the students and townsmen obeyed all their
rules, the University authorities appointed special officers
called proctors. These were more than usually clever and
energetic dons. They looked after the money and saw that
the local tradesmen did not overcharge, and they also kept
order among the students in the streets. In the Regent
House, too, they had a proper square table all to themselves
whereas the college proctor who ran God's House had not
even a round one off which to eat his dinner in hall. The

---

* Readers acquainted with the Cambridge Poets will recall the thankfulness expressed in the lines:

> Now shall the hungry seed, alive
> At last, a joyous harvest yield.
> Now shall the withered hope revive,
> And high ambition, long congealed,
> Course in the veins of gratitude.
> Here lie the paths to ease and joy
> Within the gracious latitude
> Of ducal bounty. Attaboy!

University proctors were therefore very important indeed, and although their importance has now declined, they are still worth keeping an eye on.

Sad Plight of the Modern Proctor

Nowadays the proctors have practically nothing to do because no gentleman *in statu pupillari* would dream of

Worth keeping an eye on

seriously disturbing the peace, and the tradesmen never overcharge. Also there is no money. They are therefore selected from poor and needy dons, and they just wander about the streets looking for anyone they can ravish under some pretext. Hence their new name, progs, from *prog* meaning 'to go about plundering or begging for food' Owing to the present economic situation, however—and, of course, the fact that few undergraduates now carry their food around with them—most proctors prefer a steady income to the uncertainties of what was, after all, only indiscriminate pillage, and unless the alleged offence is very serious indeed, they allow their victims to ransom themselves for the statutory unit of University currency, 6s. 8d., entertainment tax and increased cost of living included.

Cave Canem

To help them to catch their victims, the progs have real bulldogs, called 'bullers'. These are unusually fleet-footed and therefore very dangerous. University regulations say, for example, that all students must wear the old-fashioned cap and gown at night. So if a prog sees a student in brightly-coloured pyjamas, the bullers at once give chase, at the same time emitting excited little barks. (The connexion between 'hue' and 'cry', of course.) If listened to carefully, these barks sound exactly like 'Your name and college, Sir?' and the bullers themselves have been so carefully trained that although their victim says he is Mr. Bunch of Caius, or Knott of Downing, or even Servant of Jesus, they still keep on barking, and they may growl.

The authorities of the women's colleges use bull-bitches for keeping order among their students.

CHAPTER NINE

AT the end of the fifteenth century there was a more than ordinarily human don called John Fisher. He was, in fact, so very human that many people said he was a Great Humanist—which is much more so, of course. As he was, at one time and another, Master of Michaelhouse, President of Queens', Vice-Chancellor of the University and finally Chancellor for life, as well as Bishop of Rochester, he was also known as the Compleat Angler.

Fisher Hooks Erasmus

Fisher was all for the New Learning which was naturally more up-to-date than the Old, and he cleverly persuaded Erasmus to come over to Queens' and teach Greek, a language so very old that it hadn't been taught before and was therefore part of the New Learning. In Rotterdam Erasmus had already made a name for himself in the development of tooth paste, and he was also well-known as a con-

Divinely pretty, soft . . .

noisseur of good living, so his arrival in Cambridge was very important indeed.

Generous Tribute to Cambridge Girls

At Queens' Erasmus did not like the beer. It was, he said, 'raw, smal and windy', and this hurt the dons' feelings quite a lot because they were proud of their beer. But he liked the Cambridge girls. They struck him as being 'divinely pretty, soft, pleasant, gentle, and charming as the Muses'. He was particularly impressed, too, because

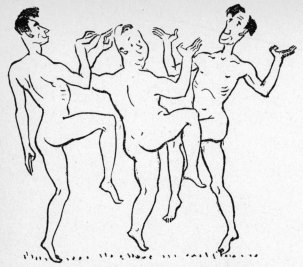

Nothing can be extracted from the naked

'they have a custom which cannot be too much admired'. 'When you go on a visit,' he said, 'the girls all kiss you. They kiss you when you arrive. They kiss you when you go away, and they kiss you again when you return.' Also this was real *osculum*.

Nowadays Cambridge girls only kiss American soldiers, but they are still just as nice.

Grecian Influence on Academic Dress

Very few students came to Erasmus's lectures because they did not like having to learn something New, but those who did were tremendously keen on the pictures of Grecian vases which he showed them, and, like the gentlemen on the vases, they took to wearing nothing at all—which, though flattering, was most irregular. Nor was Eramus altogether pleased because, as he said, when it came to collecting fees, 'nothing can be extracted from the naked'. It meant, too, that students from Newnham and Girton could not attend Greek lectures. That is why the University authorities now insist that undergraduates attending lectures must wear at least a gown of knee length.

Once they were allowed to learn Greek, the students of Newnham and Girton became just as keen as the men and tried to be like the ladies on the vases—which gave the undergraduates lots of ideas. One of them translated ἀμήχανος γυνή as 'a shiftless woman'.

Gave the undergraduates lots of ideas

Fisher Hooks Lady Margaret

Though Henry (Part VII) did not take any interest in Cambridge until he was about to die, his mother did. This was because she was Lady Margaret Beaufort who did such a lot for the University. Fisher cunningly persuaded her when he was her confessor. First of all, he said, she would have to do something about God's House which was now causing so much scandal.

American Help for Christ's

Lady Margaret had been married four times and was therefore very rich, so she was able to rebuild the college and make it bigger and more beautiful than any other, not excepting King's which, we have seen, was not nearly finished. But it was tiring work for a woman of her age, and in the end she had to get Yale supporters for her arms.

Fellows sleep two and two

This shows how willing and helpful Americans are, and also what very odd people come from Yale.

Lady Margaret's Insistence on Good Behaviour

Being a woman experienced in the ways of men, Lady Margaret was most insistent that the twelve Fellows and forty-seven scholars at Christ's should behave themselves. 'Our wish,' she said, 'is that the Fellows sleep two and two,

'Gently, gently!'

but the scholars four and four, and that no one have alone
a single chamber for his proper use.' Only a doctor might
have one to himself 'on account of the dignity of his degree'
and, of course, the fact that most doctors like to set up in
private practice.

Lady Margaret Goes into Residence

Lady Margaret also had special rooms set apart for herself
in Christ's. This was so that she could be quite sure that
everybody really did behave properly. But it made the dons
most uneasy because they knew that the presence of a woman
in college would lead to trouble. The Dean said it was bad
for discipline, and he was right. One day, when he was
rebuking a scholar in the court, she put her head out of the
window, saying: 'Gently, gently! The quality of mercy
is not strained.' That is why 'Alma Mater' has an unusual
meaning for Christ's men.

Finis Coronat Opus

Just before he died, Henry (Part VII) suddenly remembered
that nobody had done anything about King's chapel for

fifteen years, and he gave the college £5,000 so that they could put the roof on. This was a tremendous sum, and the dons, who were not expecting it, were simply staggered. This explains why the roof was not put on straight like an ordinary one.

Lady Margaret's Legacy

Being tired herself, Lady Margaret was most thoughtful about others, and she gave Fisher a chair which is still known by her name and reverently sat in by Divinity Professors. But she was wonderfully energetic for her age, and once Christ's was running properly, she readily fell in with Fisher's suggestion that she should have a college of her own.

Fisher thought John's would be a nice one to found because the old hospital of St. John was already there, and it could easily be turned into a college. Besides, the atmosphere of a hospital was bound to foster the clean-living and orderly habits for which Johnians are noted to-day. But Lady Margaret died before she could turn out the nursing staff, and when Fisher tried to do so, he got into serious trouble with the Bishop of Ely, the Archbishop of Canterbury and the Pope, as well as Cardinal Wolsey and Henry (Part VIII), all of whom were people one should not have trouble with. And when he said quite openly that he would like to 'sack the lot', they were very angry with him and never really forgave him. But he founded the college for Lady Margaret all the same, and John's men still remember her affectionately.*

Toc H Founded

While Fisher was going ahead with John's, many students became interested in combustion, and some of them, like

---

* Readers acquainted with the Cambridge Poets will recall the pride and thankfulness expressed in the lines:

> When the Johnian hair is too shaggy,
> And the Johnian pants are too baggy,
> They do not deny it.
> They proudly reply: 'It
> Is just as she wore'm, our Maggy.'

Ridley of Pembroke, Cranmer of Jesus and Gardiner of Trinity Hall, made such progress that they also became quite famous. Latimer of Clare even lit an inextinguishable candle. The origin of Toc H, of course.

Reading of Naughty Books Discouraged

This study of combustion was all part of the New Learning which was becoming more and more popular because the

Lit an inextinguishable candle

new books imported from the Low Countries were naturally rather vulgar. This worried Fisher quite a lot, and although he did not as a rule agree with Wolsey—he found his ideas woolly and irritating—he did have to admit that a public bonfire of these naughty books would be a beneficial experiment in combustion.

Fisher's Career Blocked

Fisher never agreed with Wolsey about anything else, and when Wolsey paid an official visit to Cambridge, he flatly refused to turn out and receive him—which really did annoy Wolsey because he was a Cardinal whereas Fisher was Chancellor of the University and only a Bishop. 'Who will rid me of this turbulent priest?' he cried, and when, some time later, Henry (Part VIII) heard about it, he said he would, and he had Fisher's head cut off.

Oxford Resents Cambridge Progress

Wolsey, however, was so pleased with the progress the Cambridge dons had made that he thought it a good idea to send a few to Oxford to show the dons there how to think properly. But the Oxford dons did not see it in that light, and they were very rude about it. 'Would God,' the Warden of New College said, 'that his Grace had never motioned to call any Cambridge man to his most godly college! We were clear without blot till they came.'

All-Round Brilliance of Cambridge Men

Cambridge has never been able to explain this attitude of superiority which Oxford assumes—except as evidence of an inferiority complex—because Oxford has nothing on which to base it. On the other hand, the natural brilliance of Cambridge men is seen in every walk of life. There are, for example, in addition to those already mentioned:

(1) Bacon, of Trinity, who wrote *Shakespeare*.
(2) Milton, of Christ's, the pioneer of dental hygiene.
(3) Pett, of Emmanuel, who gave the country Jane and the *Sovereign of the Seas*. (Hence Jane's *Fighting Ships*.)
(4) Herrick of St. John's and Trinity Hall, who did but see her passing by.
(5) Byron, of Trinity, a bear-flesh fancier who designed the tennis shirt.
(6) Spenser, of Pembroke, who sired a Faerie Queene.
(7) Darwin, of Christ's, who said all men are beasts.
(8) Shirley, of St. Catharine's, who invented Christian Science. ('The glories of our bloody state are shadows, not substantial things.')

and

(9) Newton, of Trinity, who discovered the gravity of things in the fall as opposed to their buoyancy in the spring.

Of these, Pett is undoubtedly the most famous, and Herrick the most fortunate.

Oxford has nothing comparable.

CHAPTER TEN

ONE thing that impressed Wolsey so much at Cambridge was the trouble the University authorities took to ensure that nobody, apart from King's men, obtained a degree if he did not deserve it. They did this, not by written examination, but by proper stand-up disputes or arguments so that the candidate couldn't possibly take it lying down merely by bringing his crib.

The Broad-Mindedness of Cambridge Men

The judge or examiner at these disputes was an 'ould bachilour'—which shows that from the very beginning the University authorities disliked any suggestion of feminine influence in educational affairs—and he sat on a tripos or three-legged stool of the type previously used at the milking

Sat on a tripos

of the examination cow. Hence the name *Tripos* for this kind of exam. Everyone spoke Latin, of course, and the candidates were taken in pairs, one maintaining the question while the other argued against it. They then changed round. That is why Cambridge men, unlike those from lesser universities, can always see both sides of a question.

Reprehensible Behaviour of Elderly Bachelors

Unfortunately, as time went on, the 'ould bachilour' took to reciting ribald verses when he should have been disputing seriously, and he had to be replaced by examiners more conscious of their duties. These were called Moderators because they toned down the verses. But they still continued with them. Hence the saying that anyone who obviously knows his stuff has been well versed.

Commendable Versatility of Tripos Examiners

The Moderators themselves were extremely clever, of course, and they suited their verses to all candidates. They could, for example, be polite:

> Young man, though you come from Sid. Sussex
> And tell us that w + x
>   Is the same as xw,
>   We say No, and must trouble you
> To confine those ideas to Sid. Sussex.

—or sympathetic:

> 'Tis a pleasure to find that in John's
> Ornithology's introduced swans.
>   But, my boy, it's a cinch,
>   When it comes to the pinch,
> Those swans are the perks of the dons.

—or ironical:

> Though your college, dear sir, may be Magdalene,
> And undoubtedly you are a lagdalene

John's Swan

Of lineage high,
We still can't see why
In your studies you did so much dagdalene.

—or sarcastic:

You would like us, O student of Clare,
To believe the components of air
Are cigarette smoke
And gases from coke,
Mixed with petrol and 'flu bugs, O yeah?

—or merely rude:

Presumptuous off-spring of Downing,
On your argument fortune is frowning.
There's a very large flaw
In your knowledge of law.
Away then, be off and stop clowning.

Clearly it is a pity that the Tripos examination is no longer conducted in verse.

Cambridge Degrees Graduated

From quite early on the University authorities recognised that, brilliant though Cambridge men are, some are more brilliant than others. So they cleverly said there should be two sorts of degrees, the normal hard one and a special or soft one. This means there are three sorts of students: those who take the hard and honest-to-God degree and become B.A. (Hon); those, the οἱ πολλοί or pollmen, who take the other; and those who fail to take either and, as the students themselves like to say, 'get ploughed'—a harrowing experience, of course.

There is, however, a fourth and most exclusive category. If the candidate does not bother to take the exam at all but stays in bed, he can still get his degree as an aegrotat, from *aeger* meaning 'sick' and *tat* (the corollary of *tit*) meaning 'this is where I laugh', because if he can pull that one off, he is rightly judged to be more than usually clever.

Examiners' Helpful Attitude

At first everybody argued with the 'ould bachilour', and because the arguments ended disastrously for many of them, they always did so on Ash Wednesdays. They could then wear sack cloth if necessary. But it was really asking too much of the pollmen who, being Greek, could never argue well in Latin, and this put the University authorities in a most awkward position because the statutes said everybody had to argue in Latin. In the end the University authorities, who are always resourceful, got over the difficulty by writing the arguments for the pollmen, like this:

RESPONDENT: *Recte statuit Doctor Strabismus, quem Deus servet.*

OPPONENT (emphatically): *Recte non statuit Doctor Strabismus, quem Deus servet.*

OPPONENT (now supporting the thesis): *Recte statuit Doctor Strabismus, quem Deus servet.*

RESPONDENT (emphatically, now opposing): *Recte non statuit Doctor Strabismus, quem Deus servet.*

MODERATOR (to Respondent): *Tu quidem, domine, optime*

disputasti. Scram. (To Opponent): *Tu quoque.* Next gentleman, please.

It was all very swift and business-like.

Grave Slur Upon Mathematicians

The introduction of mathematics as a subject for serious study was bitterly resented by theological students because hitherto they had enjoyed the exclusive performing rights of π. They said it was an 'art diabolical'—which is much worse than a diabolical art, of course—and they swore that only 'conjurers and nigromancers' could cope with it successfully, an opinion which many people still hold. Moreover, mathematicians were not nice people to know, being both 'mystical and vulgar' on account of the rude fractions they employed. So there was a lot of argument about mathematics, more so than about any other subject. That is why mathematicians are so noisy, and why the more determined among them are known as wranglers.

Petting Parties Banned on Degree Day

Students who are successful in their examinations go to the Senate House to fetch their degrees, and this is always a jolly occasion. It used to be more so for the one who came bottom in the mathematical honours list because he was presented with a large wooden spoon as well as a degree, and then chased through the town by admiring friends. But their dislike of any form

Spooning

of spooning has led the University authorities to forbid this innocent pursuit.

Simple Dignity of Admittance to Degrees

The University authorities also object to holding hands. That is why the candidate is allowed to take no more than one of the praelector's fingers when he kneels before the Vice-Chancellor to receive his degree—which shows how

Letting the dog see the rabbit

delicate everything is nowadays. Even the Latin recitation is in prose, and it is a very serious composition indeed. It raises the candidate to the degree of B.A. *in nomine Patris et Filii et Spiritus Sancti*, and nothing could be more solemn than that.

To show ordinary people that he is a real B.A. and therefore very clever, the successful candidate is allowed to wear a piece of white fur round his shoulders. This is known as 'hood-winking' or 'letting the dog see the rabbit'.

University's Keen Interest in Commerce

A B.A. is a graduate of the University, and later on, if he is sufficiently well-off and cares to apply the formula:

$$B.A. + \text{purchase price of } M.A. = M.A.$$

—he can hear another recitation and rise an M.A. without showing himself any more clever than he was when he took his B.A. But ordinary people do not know this, and to show them that he is now a real M.A. and make them think he is more clever than he was, he is allowed to wear a piece of white silk round his shoulders. This, of course, is very good for trade.

CHAPTER ELEVEN

DURING the reign of Henry (Part VIII) the University became sharply divided on the question of reforming the drill book. Many canonists wanted to continue standing at ease in the old way, but others favoured the new German method, and a decision was most important because Cambridge men have always had a big influence in world affairs.

Blue Prints Closely Studied

The naughty books which Fisher had burnt had made quite a good bonfire, but they were by no means all that had reached Cambridge, and many of the younger dons and students used to have secret readings at the White Horse Inn. This was cleverly known throughout the University as 'Germany' so that the authorities should not realise what went on there. Naturally there was a big difference of opinion over the subject matter, and this led to a dispute that grew steadily more heated until quite a number of

Books from the Low Countries—very naughty

people not only got warm under the collar but actually caught fire—which shows that the books must have been hot stuff.

Latimer's Reckless Advice

Latimer was very excited, of course, and being a Clare man and one therefore accustomed to plain speaking (*en clair*, as they say) he went so far as to preach a sermon exhorting his congregation to play trumps and win salvation —which was very remiss of him because he was well aware how touchy the University authorities were about card games and the wild play that went on in Cambridge. But what the students liked him best for was his frank statement that Greek was unworthy of a serious man's attention. So it is not really surprising that he finished by lighting an inextinguishable candle.

Henry's Great Compliment to Cambridge

The cleverness with which the University was arguing about these important questions impressed Henry (Part VIII), and as he himself was having a tricky dispute with the Pope about marriage and divorce, he thought Cranmer's suggestion that the University should decide the matter for him a particularly good one. 'Marry!' he said, the word being uppermost in his thoughts, 'I perceive that man hath the right sow by the ear.' This was just his way of saying that Cranmer had got something there. It does not mean that Cranmer kept pigs.*

Serious Issues at Stake

Henry wanted to know whether it was lawful for a man to marry his deceased brother's wife if he could not marry his deceased wife's sister, the brother and the wife being the parties deceased. This was conceded because it was unreasonable to expect any man to marry his brother's deceased wife or his own wife's deceased sister. Obviously no issue would then arise.

On the face of it, the problem did not appear very difficult because if A and B are brothers, A' and B' their wives, and a and b the wives' sisters, the multiplication sign suffices as the operative symbol of marriage to show that $A \times a$ is numerically equal to $A \times B'$ for at least nine months, so that during this period the deceased wife's sister is the same for matrimonial purposes as the deceased brother's wife, and again no issue arises. In fact, the issue arises only when it is concerned with itself, and that makes it very complicated indeed, as the dons realised. They were therefore determined to dispute as they had never disputed before, especially as they knew their failure to find the right answer would raise other and even more inconvenient issues.

* Only St. John's men have seriously gone in for farming, as readers acquainted with the Cambridge Poets will recall:

> At Cambridge the students are gowned
> In a style that betrays them to progs.
> Thus black velvet stripes are renowned
> As 'the crackling' of Johnian Hogs.

The Senate's Masterly Debate (Round One)

The Vice-Chancellor first of all had a meeting in the Regent House and proposed that the question should be left to the Doctors. This was a very clever move because the Bachelors of Divinity and the Masters of Arts at once objected on the grounds that their own valuable opinions would be left out. Moreover, those among them who thought that Henry had no lawful reason for divorcing his dead brother's wife, rightly pointed out that among the Doctors were a number who held the opposite view—which was unfair. So the Vice-Chancellor suggested a secret ballot in which everybody should say 'yes' or 'no', and this, too, was a clever proposal because everybody objected to it on the grounds that nobody would know how his friends voted.

Darkness having fallen, the meeting adjourned.

The Senate's Masterly Debate (Round Two)

Next morning, after they had said Grace, the Vice-Chancellor proposed that they should elect twenty-nine Doctors and Masters of Art to decide on a two-thirds majority what the answer should be, but nobody at all would agree. Those in favour of the divorce naturally objected to the inclusion among the twenty-nine of those not in favour, just as strongly as those not in favour objected to the inclusion of those in favour, and at first the proposal was rejected out of hand. When, however, Grace had been said again and the proposal was put a second time, the votes for and against were exactly equal, and there is no doubt that they always would have been if those in favour of the divorce had not contrived 'to cause some to depart the house which were against it'.

The Vice-Chancellor Embarrassed

Being exceptionally able men, the Doctors and Masters who were elected had no difficulty in finding the right answer, and the Vice-Chancellor himself took it to Henry at Windsor. But they did it up in two parts, and when he heard the first, which was that he should, Henry was so

pleased that he gave the Vice-Chancellor twenty real nobles
without waiting to hear the second, which was that he
shouldn't. When he heard that, he cried, 'Marry!'—
the word still being uppermost in his mind—'We are not
amused.' He was, in fact, so disconcerted that he forgot
to take back the nobles—which was a pity because, as the
Vice-Chancellor pointed out, not even a man in his position
could go round all the time trailing a retinue from the
peerage.

Terrible Slur upon a Virtuous College

Now that he knew he could count upon Cambridge, Henry
said he wouldn't have any more monasteries, but this
tried the dons very hard because it meant that they couldn't
keep their monks' college, and they liked their Benedictines.
Nor were they any happier when he gave the college to
the wicked man who had been responsible for cutting off
Fisher's head, and they were deeply shocked when the new
owner said he would re-found it as Magdalene College
because strangers to the town might easily think it was a
woman's college and not a nice one at that.

It was to hide this shame that Magdalene men took to
calling their college Maudlin.

Courtiers No Match For Dons

As soon as Henry's courtiers saw how generous he was
with the money he took from the monasteries, they thought
it a good idea to get him to do away with the colleges as well.
They would then be very rich indeed. But even though
they passed a bill for the dissolution of the colleges, they
were not nearly clever enough for the dons because the dons
cunningly arranged that the official investigators who were
supposed to report how corrupt the colleges were, should
be none other than their own Vice-Chancellor, the President
of Queens' and the future Master of Trinity, who naturally
said that the colleges were not corrupt at all. Moreover,
they dropped a note privately to the Queen asking her to
put in a word for them, and she replied that she had
'attempted the King's majesty for the stablishment of their

'Marry, I will found one myself!'

livelihood and possessions' with such success that Henry
would never do away with their colleges. 'Marry!' he
said from force of habit, 'I will found one myself.'

It was after this that all the King's friends thought they
would like to be Chancellors. As they wittily put it: *si
racquetum infringere non potes, id intra.*

CHAPTER TWELVE

TRINITY, which Henry (Part VIII) founded, is a large college
opposite Matthew's. It is called Trinity because it was
founded in three pieces, but the second piece has been lost,
and now there is only First Trinity and Third Trinity.
This does not mean that third-class students at Trinity

cannot travel first, though it does accentuate the likeness of Trinity men to rolling stock.

Seats of Learning

The building of Trinity also completed what is a recognised feature of Cambridge architecture, namely that Cambridge has no front. It is all back, just as Oxford is all side—curiosities of construction which suggest that together the two Universities at least have a bottom.

Trinity's Big Men

Henry said that Trinity was not only to be a big college:

Outsizar or very big student

it was to accommodate big people as well, and once it got going it consisted of a Master, sixty Fellows, sixty-nine scholars, sixteen sizars, six chaplains, six lay-clerks and ten boy choristers, all of whom were outstanding.

The sizars were of two kinds: outsizars or very big students who required special rations to keep up their strength, and insizars who could eat anything.

Trinity's Comprehensive Syllabus

Henry next said that, apart from being men of large build, Trinity students were to be quite different from those of other colleges. Everybody, for example, was to work really hard, and the syllabus was to include 'literature, the sciences, philosophy, good arts and sacred theology'. This meant that they had to get up very early—which at once established a marked difference. Then, for three years, they were to turn Cicero into Greek and Demosthenes into Latin, at the same time making themselves proficient in rhetoric, ethics, logic and politics—the basis of a liberal education, of course—and learning how to place the triangle ABC on the triangle DEF and even drop a perpendicular without hurting themselves, a terribly tricky business because, as everyone knows, Euclid's perpendiculars don't always fall straight down: they go sideways and even upwards. Nor was that all. For another year before passing out, they were to study Aristotle, so that if they did not pass out in the meantime, they would finish by being very clever indeed and quite unlike other students.*

Trinity M.A.s were even more clever. They learned Hebrew.

Trinity Men Easily Identified

If anybody at Trinity spoke English at times when the statutes required him to speak Latin, Greek or Hebrew, he was fined—a farthing a lapse for students and a halfpenny for B.A.s. It therefore became the custom, when conversation flagged because the speaker was unable to express himself, to say to him: '*Denarium pro sententiis.*' Nevertheless English was not neglected altogether, and from time to time the speeches in Latin and Greek which he had to make in hall on Mondays, Wednesdays and Fridays, were

---

* Readers acquainted with the Cambridge Poets will recall the conscious pride of Trinity men expressed in the lines:

O, the ignorant may jeer at what they teach us here,
Not knowing how important education is to-day.
But for them we soon will cater when we leave our Alma Mater,
With all the airs and graces of a Trinity B.A.

varied by one in English. In hall, too, he had to pin up
the Latin and Greek verses he wrote on feast days, and each
year he was usually called upon to perform in Latin and
Greek plays which the 'master of the hall' produced, and
the 'master of the hall' in addition to this saw that he was
diligent in his studies. It is not therefore surprising that
Trinity men bear a very definite hall-mark.

Loose Habits of Cambridge Students

The University authorities were very pleased about
Trinity. They felt it would set a good example to the other
students whose habits were getting rather loose. Already
they were going about in *plus quattuores*, as the new fashions
in baggy trunk-hose were called, and although there was
no longer any necessity for them to carry bows and arrows,
they frequently went crap shooting, which was prohibited.
Then, too, they not only wandered about at night making
uneven progress from bar to bar—the origin of syncopation,
of course—but they even went 'jetting', a nuisance they
were strictly forbidden to commit.

Neglectful Habits of Cambridge Dons

Nor were some of the dons any better. In spite of all
that various founders had said about being poor, austerity
feeding at high table had been largely abandoned. Masters
no longer led the members of their colleges in procession to
dispute at the schools after giving them a frugal breakfast,
and they still don't, although the custom of giving a frugal
breakfast without the subsequent dispute has been to some
extent revived. Graduates, moreover, were lax about wearing the long flowing gowns and hoods of their academic
rank, so that it was impossible at times to tell them from
disreputable townsmen; and even to-day, when discipline
has been restored, no one taking a degree would dream of
wearing a garland of roses such as students used to wear
after disputing successfully with the 'ould bachilour'.

The Townsmen Cruelly Treated

The University authorities were also having trouble with

the Mayor. They wanted him to make the streets less dangerous at night, but the Mayor said the streets were dangerous only because the unmannerly students made them so. The University, however, insisted that nobody could see where he was walking and, the Mayor's ideas on sanitation being what they were, that made the streets very dangerous indeed.

In the end they compromised. The University said the students were not to go about with 'lighted torches and links' on account of the 'great terror and apprehension they caused'—being lit up, as the saying was—and the Mayor appointed a watchman to go round after dark ordering householders to 'hang out their lights', the undoubted cause of all the respiratory trouble among the townsmen during this period.

CHAPTER THIRTEEN

WHEN Edward (Part VI) died, the Vice-Chancellor was the Master of St. Catharine's, and he was a most remarkable man even for Cambridge. Historians all agree that, although his name was Sandys, he was really made of metal.

Jane a National Figure

As it happened, this was exactly the sort of man the University wanted because a movement at once started to make Jane queen, and that was a situation which required very careful handling. The students and younger dons were all for the proposal. Hitherto they had been able to see her only in the mirror, and obviously she would be much more visible on a throne. The older dons, however, thought it would be safer if someone whose clothes were more securely fastened sat there—Mary, for example. After all, there was Alma Mater to consider. But the Duke of Northumberland, who was Chancellor, did not agree, being rather keen on Jane himself, and when he brought his army to Cambridge to arrest Mary, who was staying in the neighbourhood, he told Sandys to preach a sermon making it clear that Jane's accession could not fail to draw her admiring subjects closer to the throne.

Dr. Sandys Outwits His Enemies

Although a man of metal, Dr. Sandys was also very astute, and when the Duke told him about the sermon, he saw at once that he had to be careful.   So he cleverly asked the Lord to give him a neutral text, and the Lord opened his bible at *Joshua* i 16 where it says: 'All that thou commandest us, we will do; and whithersoever thou sendest us, we will go.'   And afterwards, in the pulpit, 'so wisely and warily he handled his words, that his enemies got not so full advantage against him as they expected'.   *In pulpito sto, sed trans murum sedeo*, as he neatly put it.

Dr. Sandys' Delicate Position

Having said he would go where he was sent, Dr. Sandys simply had to accompany the Duke and help him proclaim Jane queen on Market Hill.   But he did not like it, and when, shortly afterwards, the Duke marched out to arrest Mary and not only returned the next day 'with more sad thoughts within him than valiant soldiers about him', but made Dr. Sandys help him proclaim Mary queen, he liked the situation even less.   *Illud certe id scidit*, as he rightly observed.

Big Scenes at the Senate House

Dr. Sandys was in his office, meditating, when 'a rabble of some twenty Papists' called on him, and as they arrived without appointment and with 'railing words and violent actions', his annoyance is understandable.   In fact, he would have 'despatched some of them' with his dagger if the Doctors in attendance had not 'by their prayers and entreaties persuaded him to patience'.*

* Readers acquainted with the Cambridge Poets will doubtless recall the dramatic scene:

> Said Doctor Blythe and Doctor Bill,
>   For mercy's sake, we pray,

[*Continued at foot of next page*

Oxford's Unsporting Conduct

The University naturally had a bloody time under Mary. Twelve of the thirteen authors of a very nice Prayer Book recently published were Cambridge men, and Oxford had never done anything like that. She therefore said the two Universities should have only one Chancellor—Oxford's—and this, Cambridge thought, was definitely off-side. Nor did Oxford play fair. As fast as Cambridge made reformers, Oxford burnt them, an unfriendly thing to do in any circumstances.

Gonville in Bad Odour

The result of all this was that the University got into a very bad way indeed, and when Dr. Caius, who was visiting Cambridge, dropped into Gonville's to see how the old place was getting on—he had patronized it himself when in residence some years before—he was terribly shocked. Chapel vestments, he found, were being used as bed-covers. Holy utensils were being put to private and most improper uses. In spite of orders forbidding females to enter the premises, cows were wandering in and out at will, and he could liken the courts only to 'a stable of Augeas'. *Odorem habet*, he said, and at once made up his mind to clean the place thoroughly by taking over the management himself.

The Wide Experience of Dr. Caius

He was quite capable of doing this because he was a very clever doctor with an extensive and ever-increasing practice. At one time and another he attended all sorts of important people, among them Edward (Part VI) for *pyromania episcopa*, Mary for uncontrollable hæmorrhage, and Elizabeth

> Restrain your handys, dear Doctor Sandys,
> Be tardy of the fray.
> Dark dangers hide in homicide.
> Be not by passion led.
> So Doctor Sandys withheld his handys,
> And that way kept his head.

—which, of course, is more than the Duke of Northumberland did.

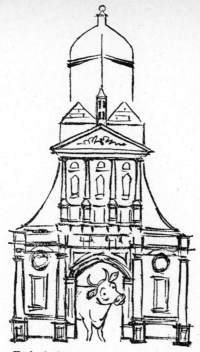

Forbade females to enter the premises

for hymeneal hallucination. He therefore knew that a doctor cannot be too careful.

Gonville Cauid Up

As soon as he had taken over the management, Dr. Caius made a lot of new rules. Nobody, he said, was to climb on to the roof except to replace a tile, or fasten a candle to a wall at any time, and on no account were chapel utensils and vestments to be used improperly. They were to be put back where they belonged immediately. And these rules applied to everyone, even dons. If they were disobedient, they would be sent down or, what was worse, put in the stocks. The result was that Dr. Caius became very unpopular indeed, especially among the dons who thought stock-taking a menial occupation, and everyone naturally became 'all caiud up', as the saying was.*

Dr. Caius Gates the Proprieties

Dr. Caius then set about enlarging the premises and extending the firm's activities. He named the gates so that the customers went in by Humility, reached Virtue, and

Thought stock-taking a menial occupation

* Readers acquainted with the Cambridge Poets will recall the jocular yet watchful attitude of the dons towards Dr. Caius expressed in the lines:

> Displaiused is Caius with what he saius.
> No busy baius seek high degraius
> On bread and chaius, but devotaius
> Of pedegraius put ill-earned faius
> On racing gaius. He now decraius
> An end to thaius. Our Australe aius
> Is a disaius his Bor'ale braius
> Will quickly fraius. By Herculaius,
> We must appaius our Doctor Caius,
> And mind, we plaius, our Qs and Paius

passed out with Honour, and to build up a really high-class business he would not allow any customers who were 'deaf, dumb, deformed, lame, confirmed invalids or Welshmen' to enter the shop. This accounts for the high principles and noticeably robust appearance of Caius men to-day.

Caius Man Discovers Jazz

To the medical side of the business Dr. Caius naturally paid a lot of attention, and as time went on some of its products became quite famous. There were, for example, Dover's Powders, Daffy's Elixir and, of course, his own

Taffy's purge

prescription, Taffy's Purge. But most important of all was Harvey's discovery of hot numbers for people feeling blue. Music, he said, was like blood because it goes round and round. This explains the bloodiness of hot music.

Popular Ignorance about Doctors

Not everybody, however, liked the way Caius ran his clinic. This did not matter while Mary was queen because she approved of blood-letting and cauterisers, but when she died, jealous doctors wrote to the papers saying his methods were old-fashioned. One even told the Archbishop of

Canterbury that Caius had 'set up a crucifix and other idols with a doctor kneeling before them', and nobody would listen when he told them that if patients only realised what they were in for when they put themselves in the hands of a doctor, they would not object when he asked Heaven for some help: they would insist that he did so.*

Deplorable Incident at Gonville & Caius

The University authorities, too, were very concerned, and in the end 'it was thought good by the whole consent of the Heads of Houses to burn the books and such other things as served most for idolatrous abuses, and cause the rest to be defaced, which was accomplished with the willing hearts, as appeared, of the whole company of that House'. Nevertheless, this deplorable incident had one good result. Since then, Heads of Houses have always avoided seriously annoying their clerks, and to-day no student would dream of burning a Master's private chattels even on a bump-supper night.

Dr. Caius' Memorable Experiment

When he was very old, Dr. Caius fell ill, and he thought he would stand a better chance of recovery if he took his nourishment as he had done as an infant. He therefore arranged that the local nursing mothers should wait upon him, but they varied so much in the quality of their supply that his moods were always changing. One day he would be 'tractable, docile and of amiable countenance', the next 'froward, peevish and full of frets'. And he died just the same.

* Readers acquainted with the Cambridge Poets will recall:

> Left to itself the flame of life may flicker.
> At the worst the patient sinks in slow decline.
> The doctor merely leads him by the quicker
> Route, and puts him underground before his time.

CHAPTER FOURTEEN

BACON was a Trinity man, but he did not write *Shakespeare* while in residence. That was because he was only twelve when he went to Trinity, and obviously had to grow up a bit before he could be properly Shakespearean.

Elizabeth's Debt to Cambridge

This happened in Elizabeth's reign, and Elizabeth could speak English because two Cambridge men, from St. John's, had taught her as a girl. Elizabethan English is thus Cambridge English, and Elizabeth herself was delighted when she read *Shakespeare* and saw that it lost none of its virility when written down. That is a further

Young Bacon

reason why she took such a personal interest in the University, and why she appointed another John's man to be her Chancellor of State. Cambridge therefore became very important indeed, especially as Lord Burghley, who was a great hurdler himself, took care that the University cleared her fences for the next forty years. The University, in fact, was definitely '*in ducatibus*', as the saying was.

Elizabeth's Concern for the Students' Welfare

Elizabeth naturally took a great interest in all that went on in Cambridge. At St. Catharine's, she said, the first-year students were not to be salted—which explains why St. Catharine's men are always so fresh nowadays—and at Peterhouse the students were on no account to go to the theatre 'lest otherwise the reputation of the scholars be cheapened, to the danger of the soul and body and to the

To the danger of soul and body

scandal of the whole House, as often arises from such exhibitions'.

Proper Play-Acting Encouraged

On the other hand, Elizabeth did not object to the illegitimate stage where she was herself a keen performer in virgin parts. At Queens', she said, the Greek Professor and the Examiner were to see that two plays were acted during the Christmas period 'lest our youths should remain rude and unpolished in pronunciation and gesture'. This explains why Queens' men always speak and deport themselves so nicely. She added, too, that the Professor and the Examiner were each to be given 6s. 8d. 'for his pains', though what the audience were to receive for theirs she did not say.

Students who refused to take part were to be punished—being kept in to write out their lines, of course.

Cambridge and the Dictators

With this ban on public entertainment the University authorities fully agreed. Like Elizabeth, they were all for some quiet fun inside the college, especially at Christmas when it could be taken in the right spirit. Trinity even went so far as to tell off a Master of Arts to see that everybody made merry with at least six 'dialogues'. (Which explains why Trinity men are so good at children's parties.) But serious plays were not neglected. The Master of Caius wrote one plainly warning Hitler and Mussolini. It was designed, he said, to 'terrify all tyrannous-minded men from following their foolish, ambitious humours'. But, unfortunately, this wicked pair never read it.

Evil Influence of the Theatre

It was only entertainment outside the colleges that the University authorities objected to. They said drolls, joggulers, tumblers, tankards, fruit machines and chorus girls diverted the students from their work. In particular they disliked Gilbert and Sullivan, not only because these disrespectful men were droll, but because they deliberately incited the students to misbehave by putting on the stage a college that might easily pass for Newnham, and then showing quite clearly that most enjoyable rewards awaited anybody bold enough to break in. The result was that the students were always trying to do so—which was very naughty of them, apart from being most disappointing to the ladies when they did not succeed.*

* Readers acquainted with the Cambridge Poets will readily recall the lines on the celebrations that followed the failure of the women to secure a share in the governing of the University and entrance to it on the same footing as men:

Weep not, sweet maid, because a bitter truth the day has brought,
And you have learned from overwhelming vote that ev'ry male,
In Cambridge now, prefers you where you are, outside the pale
Of this our University. Your schemes have come to nought,
But not your charm. Remote and radiant still, to you the crown
Of feminine allure remains. Come, then! Let's make a date
With rapture! Let's sing and dance upon the lawn! And bar no gate,
Or this ev'ning, by the living God, we'll break the damn thing down!
—as indeed they did.

The Dons Plot Against Elizabeth

Being very interested in Cambridge, Elizabeth decided to come in state and see for herself how the students were getting on, but although this was a very great honour, it alarmed the dons because they knew she had something wrong with her spleen and they had no wish to catch it. Besides, they never did like women nosing round the place. They therefore decided to keep her so busy listening to

Decided to come in state

speeches and plays in Greek and Latin and Hebrew and 'the Caldee' that she would be too tired to have a proper look round.

Elizabeth Played Out

All the Great Elizabethans were in attendance—Hawkins with the refreshments, of course—but they offered no difficulty, and as the August weather was extremely hot, they were quickly browned off. Elizabeth, however, answered all the speeches so fluently in the Latin of Cicero which her tutors had taught her that, for a time, it looked as if she would win. Moreover, on the first night she sat right through Plautus's *Aulularia* which was acted on a special stage built right across King's chapel, and on the next, a Monday, she did so with *Dido*, and on Tuesday with *Ezichias*. But this play was acted in English, and the strain of listening to a language she was not used to was too much for her, and reluctantly she had to forego 'the tragedy of Sophocles called *Ajax Flagellifer*' in Latin on the last night —being, she confessed, 'over-watched by former plays'. So the dons won after all.

The Dons Take Desperate Measures

Elizabeth never came back for a second trial of strength although she did suggest one. But by this time she had seen a lot of *Shakespeare* and, liking it very much, she also suggested that the dons should arrange a comedy in English. The dons were thus alarmed even more than they had been on the first occasion, not only because it would bring her to Cambridge again, but because the idea of a comedy in English was utterly repugnant to them. It was so repugnant, indeed, that they said it simply couldn't be done—if only for the reason that they had 'no practice in the English vein'. So they proposed one in Latin instead. 'Marry!' said Elizabeth. 'Not me!'

The University Dresses Fashionably

Although she did not come to Cambridge again, Elizabeth never lost interest in the University, and she was always giving it things. She gave it some new statutes to replace the old ones, which were worn out, and she also said it could wear a new coat with proper arms in it. *Gules a cross ermine and four gold leopards with a book gules upon the cross*, was her description of the coat, but it doesn't really mean anything more than that a cross marks the spot where the book is to be found.

Oxford thought this very funny. Obviously, they said,

learning at Cambridge is a closed book. 'But,' Cambridge retorted, 'yours is always open at the same page. *Ridete illud ab, si potestis!*'

CHAPTER FIFTEEN

AT this period there were more famous men at Cambridge than usual because Oxford had stopped burning them. Trinity, for example, had a Master named Whitgift who was so clever that he became an archbishop without knowing any Greek, and before that Corpus had one named Parker who was even more clever because he got away not only with Canterbury but with a piece of Cambridge as well.

Unexpected Knowledge of a Queens' Don

Queens', too, had an exceedingly clever President named Chaderton who knew all about women—which, for a don, was most unusual, dons being unmarried, of course. During a wedding sermon he said 'that the choice of a wife is full of hazard, not unlike as if one in a barrel full of serpents should grope for one Fish; if he 'scape harm of the snakes and light on a fish, he may be thought fortunate, yet let him not boast, for perhaps it may be but an Eel'. In fact, the best one can ever hope to catch is an old trout.

Remarkable Character of Dr. Perne

But most important of all the famous men at Cambridge during this period was Spenser.

Although Spenser was only sixteen and far from being full grown when he went up, it was recognised at once that he would be a very big man. That is why he entered Pembroke as a sizar. Even so, he outgrew his strength and was frequently ill. The dons then allowed him sick benefit at the rate of 6s. 8d. for every four weeks of time off. Nevertheless, in spite of this kindness, Spenser did

Perhaps it may be but an eel

not really like dons. He thought them old-fashioned and argued with them, even with the Vice-Chancellor, Dr. Perne, who was naturally a most remarkable man, being 'a morning book-worm and afternoon malt-worm, a right juggler, as full of sleights, wiles, fetches, casts of leger-de-main, toys to mock apes withal, odd shifts and knavish practices as his skin can hold'. This, however, is not to say that Dr. Perne was always tight.

Wonder Child Born to Spenser

Spenser was particularly interested in eugenics, and having a close view of the Cambridge girls, he was able to see for himself how far attractiveness is hereditary. But he did not produce his *Faerie Queene* until he had gone down. The Pembroke regulations would not allow him to do anything like that in college.

Able to see for himself

Concern for the University's Fair Name

Then there were Greene and Nash (of St. John's) and Marlowe (of Corpus) who became the 'roaring boys' of London. Hence, of course, 'literary lions'. They were, too, not particularly outstanding. As Greene said in his autobiography: 'Being at the University I light among wags as lewd as myself with whom I consumed the flower of my youth.'

The University authorities were most concerned about these goings-on because they were giving Cambridge not only a bad name but one it did not really deserve, among the students being a number who were quite decent young men.

That is why Sir Walter Mildmay, who was a Christ's man and therefore very holy, said he would found a college where lewd wags would not be allowed.

Emmanuel Not Allowed to Wag

Sir Walter was most determined about this. He said the 'idle gossip of youths' was not only a 'waste of time' but also a 'bad habit for young minds'. So he would not allow anybody in his college to talk, except under adequate supervision. Furthermore, this would ensure the purity of their speech. Then, to check any naughtiness in other directions, he said the dons were to go round the dormitories at least twice a week at night and 'carefully examine' what the students were doing. If they were talking or being otherwise naughty, the Dean was to whip them.*

Nor was that all. In addition to chapel attendance and 'frequent hearing of sermons', bachelors as well as students were to say prayers with their tutors each night at eight o'clock, and every Sunday afternoon at three the Dean was to catechise the whole College. This explains why Emmanuel men are so pure-minded, devout and peace-loving to-day.

Elizabeth Approves of Emmanuel

When Elizabeth heard about it all, she was very disturbed and sent for Sir Walter and accused him of 'erecting a Puritan foundation'. 'Madame,' he replied, 'I have set an acorn, which when it becomes an oak, God knows what will be the fruit thereof.' 'Oak, eh?' she said.

The Townsmen's Clever Move

Now that the University was so important, the authorities were more anxious than ever to make the townsmen do

---

* Readers acquainted with the Cambridge Poets will recall the lines:

> To the freshman who talked in Emmanuel,
> The Dean said: 'For that I shall tan you well.'
> But the young man just chose
> To punch the Dean's nose.
> 'Tan me well, did you say? . . . Can you hell!'

what the University wanted. But the townsmen were still unwilling to obey anyone except themselves, and they cunningly persuaded the Lord Lieutenant of the County to be High Steward of the Borough because he was, they knew, a personal friend of Elizabeth's and therefore just as powerful as anybody the University could produce, Moreover, they sent such a lot of nice things, like household earthenware and bed linen, to his house at Kirtling that he was quite glad to be High Steward of the Borough, and he said that nobody was to be rude to the Mayor any more—which was most serious because, as we have seen, the University always had been rude to the Mayor. So when a student forgot himself and used 'evyll and foule words' to the Mayor shortly afterwards, Lord North at once ordered 'the varlet' to be put in the stocks and have one ear nailed to them. This pleased the townsmen tremendously, of course, and their cry of 'Ear, Ear!' has become generally used to signify approval.

The Students Refuse to Be Intimidated

This did not mean that the students' speech became any less robust. As they themselves said, even a gold leopard cannot change its gules. Lord North's action merely discouraged them from interfering with the Mayor while he was High Steward. It did not prevent them from being rude to anyone else. And so it has remained. Titus Oates, a Caius man, once rebuked his tailor with 'horrid imprecations', setting thereby a fashion which is still popular; and when George Fox came to the town, he was most impressed by what he heard. 'I passt to Cambridge yᵗ eveninge,' he said, 'and when I came into ye tounde ye schollars was uppe hearinge of mee: and was exceedinge rude. . . . They was exceedinge rude in ye Inn and in ye Courtes and in ye streetes.'

Chesterton Declared 'Persona Non Grata'

In addition to disliking the Mayor and Lord North, the University authorities also disliked Chesterton.

Chesterton, they said, 'hath and doth continually annoy

our University'. This was largely because the students liked billiards, which Chesterton was famous for, and they were always going over to play although the authorities had quite definitely said they were not to. As the authorities put it, they were dead against 'the attempts of light and decayed persons'—a most unfriendly description of Chesterton, of course—'for filthy lucre to devise and set up in open places shewes of unlawfull, hurtfull, pernicious and unhonest games' within five miles of Cambridge.

Later, when James (Part I) said these games were to include 'loggets and nine-holes', Chesterton meant still more to both the students and the townsmen because

Unkind to the bear

nobody could then ride out to the Gogs for a round of golf.

The University authorities did not mind Milton.

The Townsmen Express Their Resentment

The townsmen in particular were most annoyed about all this, and when the Vice-Chancellor sent a proctor and a bedell to stop them from baiting a bear during sermon time one Sunday afternoon, they were so angry that they threw the bedell to the bear 'in such sort that he could hardly keep himself from hurt'.

The R.S.P.C.A. Inspector agreed with the Vice-Chancellor. It was unkind to the bear.

Chesterton's Unsporting Behaviour

Chesterton also had a football team, and when the University went there to play, the home side were still so resentful of the Vice-Chancellor's attitude that they deliberately 'hid divers staves secretly in the church porch' and, choosing a moment when the visiting players were not looking, laid about their heads with such vigour that many of them had to 'run through the river' in order to escape. Hence the origin of Lacrosse and the exhortation to 'get cracking'.

CHAPTER SIXTEEN

THE students of Emmanuel College attracted a lot of attention because they were so different from all the other students. Moreover they were such nice young men that women found them quite irresistible. That is why Lady Francis Sidney said she would like to found a pure college too.

Sidney Sussex Undernourished

Lady Francis was a widow, of course, but her husband, the Earl of Sussex, had left her only £5,000; and this was not really enough. For some time, therefore, Sidney Sussex was smaller than she intended. On one occasion, indeed, it could not enter its boat for the May Races because the students were all taking degrees, and on another, although it raced most successfully, it only just managed to do so because there were no more than ten students in the whole college.*

Nevertheless her executors cleverly made the £5,000 do for a start by turning the Grey Friars malthouse into the college chapel. The mellowness of the singing at Sidney

* Readers acquainted with the Cambridge Poets will recall the lines commemorating this occasion:

> There were eight to row and one to steer,
> And one to run on the bank and cheer.

Sussex was thus assured, and it was with genuine regret that a new chapel had to be built afterwards.

Alarming Mortality among Donors

When they saw how important and influential the University was, ambitious people tried to curry favour by giving it presents.   The Earl of Essex began by presenting a magnificent silver cup, but this did not really work because, although he became Chancellor, Elizabeth cut off his head two years later.   The Duke of Buckingham, too, gave the University three lovely nutmegs for the bedells to carry, but a disappointed naval officer killed him, and the Earl of Holland who followed Buckingham as Chancellor and gave another nutmeg, was duly beheaded by Cromwell.   This discouraged intending donors quite a lot, and nowadays people think it safer to make presents to the University after they are dead.

When James (Part I) came to the throne, he gave the University two seats in parliament, but this, being an unfriendly act, put his life in no danger.

Watch Committees Foreshadowed

As soon as Lord North was dead and it was safe to be rude to the Mayor again, the Clare students were very naughty indeed.   They wrote a play making fun of the Mayor, and then not only invited the Mayor and all the leading townsmen and their wives, but put them in seats from which they could not withdraw until they had seen it—which shows how lax Clare had become because its statutes definitely said the students were to be 'docile, proper and respectable'. Clare, in fact, became so famous for its naughty plays that James (Part I) twice went to see one of them which made fun of lawyers, and 'laughed exceedingly' although the Lord Chief Justice 'glanced at the scholars with much bitterness'.

Move to Refine Undergraduate Behaviour

All this greatly annoyed the pure students in other colleges, as well as the Mayor and the Lord Chief Justice.

They said it was 'in for a dig'—more suitable, that is, for a common lodging house than a proper college—and as their numbers were now quite large, the University authorities had to take some notice of what they said. Also there were some very important men among them. One was Oliver Cromwell.

Cromwell's Unrestrained Youth

Sidney is particularly proud of Cromwell because no other college has produced a real dictator. To show this, the dons keep a picture of him in the hall which must be exactly like him since he told the painter to 'remark all these roughnesses, pimples, worts, and everything as you see me'. The college register, too, describes him as *grandis ille impostor, carnifex perditissimus*, and nothing could rate him more highly than that. But the dons never liked him very much, personally, because he was 'one of the chief matchmakers'

The Dons never liked him very much

and they were naturally all against undergraduates getting married. In addition he captained the football and cudgel teams—which was a very wicked thing too. As he himself afterwards admitted: 'I was a chief, a chief among sinners.'

'The Lady of Christ's'

Knowing that Cromwell would want a clever secretary later on, another important man named Milton came up to Christ's. He studied dental hygiene and horticulture. His mulberry tree is very famous, of course. It is one of 300 which the college bought from James for 18s. some

Here we go Round the Mulberry Bush

years before—the other 299 unfortunately died—and it grows 'in a certeyn parcell of Grounde lying in the bakeside of the said Collegge'.

Milton was very beautiful to look at, and as the students seldom had a bath in those days, his sex was a matter of speculation for some time.

Milton's Keen Sense of Humour

Although he was very pure, Milton always saw the funny side of things, and it amused him to write merry verses about them.   Some of these, such as *Here we go round the Mulberry Bush* and his description of Hobson's death, have become quite well-known.

Hobson was the famous stable proprietor and water engineer, and his death at the age of nearly ninety in the middle of a plague struck Milton as being very funny indeed because Hobson himself had no choice this time.*

Cambridge Blockaded

As a rule the University was not seriously worried by the plague because most dons and students were in a sweat anyway. (The term 'swotting' derives, of course, from *sweat, swat, swot*.) But on this occasion it interfered with the students' work so much that it was really serious.   Some colleges had to close down altogether.   Others shut themselves up and allowed only the dons to go out, and Christ's thought the situation so alarming that they brought three women into the college—a laundress and two bedmakers— an unheard of thing although they 'appointed them a chamber to lie in together'.   The Vice-Chancellor, too, lived all by himself in Corpus, 'a destitute and forsaken man'.   This isolation, however, proved most effective, especially as, on the principle of starving a fever, the neighbouring farmers shut up Cambridge itself.

Grave Concern for the University's Health

Milton was naturally interested in the health of his Alma Mater.   'She vomits now of sickness,' he said, 'but ere it be well with her, she must vomit of strong physic.'   And with this Cromwell agreed.   He diagnosed the King's Evil and favoured the purge, and when the townsmen cunningly

---

* Readers acquainted with the Cambridge Poets will remember:

Osses, eh? Oh, yes, I've osses—plenty, aye, and more
To suit the like o' thee.   (Saddle Bess, Charley—by the door.)
What's that?   Thee'll look around?   Well, do.   But also look'ee 'ere.
Old Hobson's rule has been the same for nigh on forty year.
The oss that stands by stable door's the oss that next goes out,
And mark'ee well, if 'ee don't like, then 'ee can go without.
No man says what he'll do in 'ere while Hobson has a voice.
So make'ee mind up.   Take or leave it.   That's old Hobson's choice.

elected him M.P. for Cambridge, the dons were definitely worried. And so were the students who clearly saw the danger of being rude to the Mayor.

The Dons Decide to Support the King

Cromwell's election as M.P. for the Borough naturally forced the dons to side with the King because they couldn't possibly support anyone who supported the Mayor. As they explained, if they really did have the King's Evil, obviously the Royal Touch was the thing to cure it. So they were all for Charles (Part I) and heartily agreed with him that Parliament ought to be made to get off its rump— an undignified posture, anyhow.

A little tedious

Ingenious Use for Head-Covering

Charles liked to see how loyal the University was, of
course, but he found their devotion, when expressed in
Latin and Greek and Hebrew, just a little tedious.   So one
day he sent his young son, who was to be Charles (Part II).
The dons, however, were just as loyal to him, and he, too,
was most appreciative.   At the comedy performed in
Trinity 'he gave all signs of great acceptance which he could,
and more than the University dared expect', and they were
so pleased that they made him an M.A. although he was
only eleven.   Then they took him to King's chapel, and
he said his prayers at the entrance to the choir stalls and
'was so little ashamed that, in the midst of that multitude,
he hid not his devotion in his hat'—which shows that even
in those days people used to talk through their hats.

The Mayor's Mean Theft

At this point Charles (Part I) stated quite definitely that
he'd had enough of Parliament, and everybody in Cambridge
was most excited, especially the townsmen because Cromwell
said he was going to captain the Parliamentary side.   They
were, in fact, so pleased that they fired their muskets at the
college windows.   This annoyed the students because it
prevented them from working, and they at once ordered
some muskets for themselves.   But when the muskets
arrived in Cambridge, the Mayor cunningly stole ten of
the fifteen cases so that it became more dangerous than
ever to be rude to him.

Cromwell Doesn't Play Fair

The trouble began when Charles asked the University to
pass round its plate and collect some money for him.   His
idea was that all the colleges should put something in for
him because, if they did, he would be far richer than
Cromwell.   But Cromwell's idea was to take something
out when the plate came his way, and he was so clever that
he often succeeded in taking the plate as well.   That is
why the University is so short of mess-traps to-day.

Cromwell's Inconsiderate Behaviour

To prevent anything like this happening again, Cromwell not only put a lot of roundheads in the town but billeted them in the colleges, and this really annoyed the University because there wasn't a bump of intelligence among them. They scrounged everything they could, broke all the nice furniture, burnt all the beautiful carved woodwork in the rooms, and did no end of thoughtless damage—just as soldiers always do. Then they used King's chapel as a drill-hall and destroyed the splendid bridges along the Backs, and at St. John's they even turned one court into a prison for the dons they didn't like. Into this Cromwell put the Master of Sidney, a thing that shocked the University more than any of his other misdeeds because no Cambridge man had ever treated an old master like that. It was a proper frame-up, they said.

The colleges did what they could to keep going, of course, but they were in a very bad way. Clare could raise no more than 10s. for securing 'the favour of the Lord Protector'.

Dowsing the Light Divine

The dons were hardly less annoyed over Cromwell's appointment of Dowsing to put out the sacred light. Most colleges had a number of angels on their books and were very proud of them, and this severance of the celestial connexion was therefore a cruel blow. Dowsing was so thorough too. Even if they disguised themselves as stained glass, he turned them out. And not only angels. At St. Catharine's he would not allow George to stay with his dragon, and the plight of this unhappy pair in their trek about the country is shown by the number of public houses in which they had to stay.

The Townsmen's Domineering Behaviour

After Cromwell had won the match at Naseby, the townsmen were more insolent than ever. They threw stones and other things at the students in the streets, and they wouldn't let the dons say anything against Parliament even in academic disputes. Both dons and students bitterly resented this, and on one occasion when the townsmen broke in and seized the Orator and the Moderator as well, a great battle followed. But although the Trinity students 'did gallantly', the townsmen won.

The Mayor, too, was just as offensive. He rescued

Over-zealous

George Fox when the students were being rude to him, and he quite spoiled everybody's fun by putting his cloak round a zealous Quaker who was preaching in the streets without any clothes on.

CHAPTER SEVENTEEN

WHEN Charles (Part II) came to the throne, the University was very pleased for several reasons. He said all the Masters and dons who had been expelled could go back if they wanted to, and if they didn't, they could become bishops. Colleges, too, could have proper feasts just as they used to have, and they could even teach Latin and Greek again if anyone cared to learn them. But most of all the University liked the return of its old privileges because the students could now be rude to the Mayor once more.

Emmanuel Decides to Emigrate

Although Charles wanted everybody to be merry, and the University as a whole willingly obliged, Emmanuel dons were most unhappy. Having provided no less than seven

They called their ship the *Mayflower*

pure Masters to replace the impure ones whom Cromwell removed, they regarded these changes not only as a slight upon themselves but as evidence that Charles did not wish the University to be pure.   So it was clearly no place for them.   That is why so many Emmanuel men emigrated to America where the Mann Act is specially designed to make men pure.

They called their ship the *Mayflower* because there was still hope.

Phi-Beta-Kappa Exported

John Harvard was an Emmanuel man, and as he couldn't take Emmanuel to America with him, he decided to build a college over there, but he was so clever that he built a whole University, not just a college, for only £779 17s. 2d. His knowledge, too, of the Greek alphabet had a deeply fraternal influence on American student life which soon modelled itself on such well-known societies as the ψs bridge club at St. John's, the $\phi\tau$ air squadron and, of course, the Cats' μs

New Parlour Game Invented

Now that the dons and students could enjoy themselves again, the University quickly produced its normal output of remarkable men.   Among these was a Master of Trinity whose name was Barrow.

Once, when Dr. Barrow was Court Chaplain, the Earl of Rochester foolishly tried to get the better of him, saying: 'Doctor, I am yours to the shoe-tie.'

'My Lord,' said Barrow, 'I am yours to the ground.'

'Doctor, I am yours to the centre.'

'My Lord, I am yours to the Antipodes.'

'Doctor, I am yours to the lowest pit of Hell.'

'There, My Lord, I leave you.'

This form of dialogue was very popular after the Restoration, and in honour of the Merry Monarch was known as 'Poking Charley'.

Dr. Barrow's Unflagging Humour

Dr. Barrow enjoyed himself most of all preaching sermons

longer than anyone else.   After they had lasted four hours,
it became the custom for the organist to play a voluntary
—the *Nunc Dimittis*, of course—but it was no good.

Mathematicians Encouraged

Dons and students, in fact, were now enjoying themselves
so much that even their mathematics ceased being pure.
Barrow applied his to rotary motion—hence the wheel-
barrow—and when people saw how useful this was, they
realised there was more in mathematics than they thought,
and that mathematicians might invent all sorts of useful
things if properly encouraged.   That is why Lucas, who
always wanted light on dark matters, made Dr. Barrow
comfortable in a special chair.

Newton's Amazing Mind

When Dr. Barrow got up, an even more remarkable
Trinity man sat down.   His name was Newton, and he had
a marble mind—which was most interesting because nobody
had ever heard of anyone with a marble mind before.
Marble heads, yes—and ivory domes.   But now marble
minds.   Also it used to go on voyages round strange seas
of thought, and every time it came back, Newton reduced
something else to a formula.   One day it was academic
degrees.   An M.A., he said, was obviously equal to the
force P—a constable, in fact—so that a B.A. ranked at the
best as a mere special.

It was all very disconcerting.

Strenuous Nature of Mathematics

As long as 'x' remained to be found, Cambridge men
were determined to find it, and so many tried, with such
terrible effects upon their health and appearance, that
before long mathematics was definitely classified not only
as one of the Inhumanities but as an unhealthy trade.
Indeed, a Sidney student said that when he went to argue
with the examiners about Newton and the hiding place of
'x', one of the candidates fainted at the outset, several
'declined the contest from mere debility', and 'most of

those who did endure to the end looked more like worn-out rakes than men under three-and-twenty in the bloom of youth and the pride of manhood'. Mathematical students are therefore picked out easily from those who take the less exacting and Humane triposes.

The Dons Play a Classical Trick

Although the search for 'x' was really the problem, so

Suavium

many students began looking for it that their very numbers set the University authorities another because there was hardly anybody left to learn Latin and Greek. Several of the classical dons therefore started a Platonic School. This, they said, was bound to be popular because its members could do no wrong. If, for example, one of them took a girl up the Granta in a punt, it was *suavium*, but if a mathematical student did so, that was *osculum*. Many students as well as dons thus became Platonists, but the School did not last long. As the mathematicians said, this thing should be impossible.*

Pepys's Praiseworthy Industry

Another outstanding Cambridge man at this time was Pepys. At Magdalene, where he studied Optics and did much research in Double Vision during the Commonwealth, he earned a reputation for never sparing himself, and on one occasion had to be 'solemnly admonished' in the presence of all the Fellows 'for having been scandalously overserved the night before'.

Disastrous Result of Overwork

The Fellows also gave themselves very seriously to their own researches, and Pepys often came back to Cambridge to help them at the 'Three Tuns' and the 'Rose'. Most industrious of all, though, was the Master. In the end his health suffered so much that the Archbishop of Canterbury had to warn him not to work so hard—sober advice which the Master took to the extent of abstaining through four whole days. But he died in consequence. That is why Magdalene has a motto above the entrance to the dining-hall which says *Garda ta Foye*—meaning, of course, 'Mind your liver'.

Charles Rebukes the Dons

Being an M.A. himself, Charles (Part II) was very proud of Cambridge, and he liked all his important guests to go there and see for themselves what a splendid place it was, especially as the Wrens were doing so much building for the colleges. (Which shows, incidentally, how old and

---

* Readers acquainted with the Cambridge Poets will remember:

> Said the student of Plato: 'I think
> In rapturous embrace to sink
>   Is unworthy of Cupid.'
>   Cried his girl: 'Don't be stupid.
> That's a new one on me. Strike me pink!'

Gave themselves very seriously to research

versatile this auxiliary naval service is.) He was therefore most particular about the way the dons received their visitors, and he said their 'supine and slothful habit of reading their sermons' must stop. He liked them 'by memory and without book'. They were shorter that way.

The Dons Terribly Mortified

Even so, things went wrong at times, and when the Ambassador from the Emperor of Morocco came—'a pretty lusty man with a swarthy complexion'—he was so upset by the soused eels they fed him on that he recovered barely in time to receive his M.A. But nothing proved so distressing to the dons as the Grand Duke of Tuscany's visit, for after listening to all their sermons and speeches, he said he understood their Latin even less than their English.

CHAPTER EIGHTEEN

In order that the University should not be interrupted by any change in State policy, the authorities cleverly arranged that each college should have three Masters, one Puritan, one Papist and one Protestant. They could then change round as required. There was thus no interruption when Charles (Part II) removed the Puritans and restored the Protestants. Nor was there when James (Part II) installed the Papists and William (Part III) put back the Protestants. This was known as 'Keeping the Ps'. Anne, however, did not make any changes, and the Trinity dons had, in consequence, to try to get rid of Dr. Bentley themselves.

Trinity's Lack of Harmony

Being a John's man, Dr. Bentley did not think much of Trinity. To put matters right, he made all the dons take degrees in divinity, fined them if they did not go to chapel, and to raise money for a new organ, said he would not allow any more college feasts. But this only produced sharp discord, and when he tried to divide the college income so that he got a bigger share, even the organist refused to play any more.

Trinity Dons Decline to Shell Out

But what annoyed the dons most was being called upon to pay for the new Master's Lodge which Bentley had built and fitted with all modern conveniences (such as coal fireplaces and ceilings), especially as he was very rude indeed when they hesitated. He would not even let the Junior Bursar have anything to eat because he objected to the hen-house. 'Scramble,' Bentley said, 'and no poaching.'

That is why the dons said they were simply egged on to get rid of him.

The Battle of Bentley

As the object was to decide who should be thrown out of Trinity, this battle was fought in chukkas.

First Chukka. The dons won this easily, but the Bishop of Ely, who was acting as umpire, unfortunately died before he could give Bentley out.

Second Chukka. This Bentley won. When George (Part III) visited Cambridge, Bentley made some money on the side by selling honorary degrees to his retinue at four guineas each, but one man cunningly demanded his money back, and the University authorities, hearing that Bentley had done this undignified thing, took away all his degrees. He sued them, however, in the King's Bench, and they had to return them.   So he continued to be Master.

Third Chukka.   This went to the dons, but although the new Bishop of Ely lived long enough to give Bentley out, Bentley just would not go, and as the Vice-Master, who was the official chucker-out on these occasions, refused to do any chucking, and nobody could make him, Bentley still continued to be Master.   So the dons never really won the battle after all.

Stuffy Atmosphere at Trinity

Uffenbach, who was in Cambridge for a time during the battle, liked Bentley.   He said he spoke 'good and tolerably intelligible Latin'.   But he did not care much for Trinity, the hall of which was 'very large, but ugly, smoky, and smelling so strong of bread and meat' that he couldn't possibly eat anything in it.

Formal Lectures Unpopular

Uffenbach was also 'amazed that no courses of lectures were delivered' in the University, and that 'only in the winter three or four lectures are given by the professors to the bare walls, for no one comes in'—which shows that the students were just as wise then as they are now.*

Dangers of Mere Book-Learning Avoided

This attitude does much to explain the neglected state of the various libraries. At Gonville & Caius Uffenbach found the library housed in 'a miserable garret under the roof', and as the top step leading to it was buried in pigeon dung and the manuscripts lay thick with dust on the floor, he deduced that it was 'scarcely ever visited or not at all'. At

Waters are running at Trumpington Mill

Magdalene 'all the books with hardly one exception' were 'entirely overgrown with mould', and at Peterhouse they were so covered with dust that he had to borrow a towel from the librarian and use it as a pinafore, only to discover they were 'sorry stuff' after all. This, of course, disposes of any suggestion that Cambridge men were ever bookworms.

* Readers acquainted with the Cambridge Poets will recall the lines which so adequately put the students' point of view:

When the winds are blowing on Madingley Hill,
And the waters are running at Trumpington Mill,
What does it matter to you,
    And what does it matter to me,
That Cæsar conquered Gaul in B.C. 53?

The Mayor Deeply Offended

As for Cambridge itself, Uffenbach said that, apart from the colleges, it was 'one of the sorriest places in the world', and the Mayor agreed. As he pointed out, only in one of the sorriest would the Mayor not be allowed to preside in his own guildhall. This was because, not long before, he had asserted himself and 'denied unto the Vice-Chancellor the precedence in the joynt seat at the upper end of the guildhall . . . which refusal was the occasion of a great deal of contempt and indignity offered by some rude persons to the said Vice-Chancellor', and the University authorities had forced him to apologise by refusing to buy anything from the townsmen. This, however, is not conclusive evidence that Cambridge invented the strike weapon.

Never recognised by the Board of Extra Mural Studies

Public Examinations Instituted

The students were particularly hurt by the Mayor's attitude because they were doing their best to improve education in the town, even to the extent of holding public examinations in Petty Cury where they often used to 'set women on their heads at noonday'. Unfortunately this simple method of teaching women to see things the right way up has never been recognised by the Board of Extra Mural Studies.

Gray Made a Butt Of

A very important Cambridge man at this time was Gray. He was a very sombre poet and therefore took a dim view of everything. His rooms at Peterhouse, he said, 'were noisy, and the people of the house dirty', and they were so careless with their matches that, as a precaution, he fastened a rope to his window for, he explained, 'my neighbours every day make great progress in drunkenness'. They naturally did not like this. So they put a large tub of water underneath, and one night, when they shouted 'Fire!' Gray slid right into it. Even the Master laughed then, and Gray was so mortified that he left Peterhouse and went to Pembroke where the students are better behaved.*

Peterhouse acquired its name 'Pothouse' not from these convivial excesses but from Gray's habit of growing mignonette in a window-box while he was there.

Carefree Spirit Abroad

Gray did not really like Cambridge. It was, he thought, too cheerful and undignified. The Master of Pembroke rode about the pond in his garden on a water-bicycle, and the students at large used to 'game in coffee-houses on

---

* Readers acquainted with the Cambridge Poets will remember that Gray afterwards recalled this incident in his *Ode on the Nearby Prospect of Peterhouse*:

> Ye pseudo towers, ye fell facade,
> That shield yon watery butt,
> Where once my fearful manhood strayed
> And, plummet-like, I plunged—phut.

Sundays', a thing they would never do now that gaming is permitted from Monday to Saturday. Nor would the modern don ever dream of pawning his fellowship to a moneylender and then taking only half the advance in wine and cigars, as a King's don did. He would take it all.

Abyssinian Emperor at King's

Nevertheless a certain number of dons and students were very serious-minded indeed. At one time Magdalene took

A little Negus

life so earnestly that there was some danger of the river becoming choked with tea-leaves. At King's, too, the dons as a whole were never given to hasty action. When the Whigs and Tories both entered candidates to make a three-cornered election, they took thirty-one hours to choose their Provost although they could not leave the chapel until they had done so—which was terribly inconvenient because there was a heavy frost that night and by two o'clock in the morning there were 'some wrapped in blankets, erect in their stalls like mummies; others asleep in cushions like so many gothic tombs; here a red cap over a wig; there a face lost in the cape of a rug. One blowing a chafing dish with a surpliced sleeve; another warming a little negus'—who felt the cold horribly, of course.

Source of The Granta

Then the students were so attracted by the magazines they read in the coffee-houses that they cleverly wrote one of their own, and they called it the *British Apollo* because it was all about themselves and no other title seemed adequate. And they still write about themselves although they now call their magazine *The Granta*. But it is still just as clever and certainly more jolly.

CHAPTER NINETEEN

ALTHOUGH Cambridge men easily maintained their high position in the academic world throughout this period, they did not at times show their true brilliance. That is because they were given to over-eating, which was bad for their figures, and their mathematics fell off in consequence. Then they went in a lot for bowls, not caring much for cricket and football, and also for punting, Newmarket being so handy; and they did all sorts of unacademic things like carpentry. The Trinity dons, indeed, were 'notorious for their vices'.

Self-Sacrificing Attitude of the Dons

Nevertheless, the very fact that the dons seldom did anything by halves—preferring round figures, of course—set a splendid example to the students. When they opened Stourbridge Fair, the University officials and the Vice-Chancellor always dined there, having a large dish of herrings, a roast neck of pork, a plum pudding, a boiled leg of pork, a pease pudding, a goose, a huge apple pie and a round of beef 'with ale and bottled porter in great profusion'. Before they started, the Senior Proctor provided cakes and wine at the Senate House. Most students, therefore, profiting by this demonstration, had no difficulty in passing out.

Brilliance of Cambridge Men Affirmed

To mention only a few of the important men at Cambridge during this period, there were:

(1) Porson, of Trinity, the craven scholar and conscientious objector.

Round figure

(2) Richard Watson, of Trinity, the original 'Clever Dick'.
(3) Pitt, of Pembroke, who rolled up the map of Europe.
(4) Sterne, of Jesus, whose novel ideas resulted in Shandy.
(5) Addenbrooke, of St. Catharine's, who never married yet produced Addenbrookes.
(6) Simeon, who preached the divine right of King's.
(7) Paley, whose evidence supported Christ's.
(8) Wordsworth, of St. John's, who said the pen is mightier than the sword.

(9) Coleridge, of Jesus and the 15th Dragoons, who said it wasn't and wanted everybody to wear pants.

Porson's Determination to Live in Peace

Porson was a very remarkable man indeed.   In addition to being a craven scholar, he objected so conscientiously to taking orders that Trinity had to deprive him of his fellowship although he definitely had a sociable disposition.*

Watson's Anxiety to Help

Richard Watson, who was actually a mathematician, was an unusually obliging man.   He undertook the duties of Chemistry Professor although, as he said, he 'had never read a syllable of the subject, nor seen a single experiment in it', and he did not study theology at all until he was elected Regius Professor of Divinity.   Then they made him Bishop of Llandaff.

As Holmes himself said: 'By heavens, Watson, this is marvellous!'

Pitt Never Foxed

Pitt was so brilliant that, although he was only fourteen when he entered Pembroke, the authorities knew at once that it was no use arguing with him.   That is why they let him have his M.A. without any dispute at all, and why people still talk about being 'pitted against' anyone who is more than usually tough.   As befitted his youth, he was always very sober, drinking port in moderation whereas Fox, his rival, preferred claret in excess.   But he developed into quite a man of the world—he read geography, of course —and in the end was able to roll up the map of Europe, having no further use for it.

When he died, his many admirers built the Pitt Press as

---

* Readers acquainted with the Cambridge Poets will remember Porson's confession:

> I went to Strasbourg where I got drunk
> With that most learned Professor Brunck.
> I went to Wortz where I got more drunken
> With that more learned Professor Rhunken.

a memorial, and to show the relation between quires and places where they sing, they made it exactly like a church.

Sterne Facts

Sterne was another brilliant man. At Jesus he read subjects as wide apart as applied mathematics (as far as the mechanics of sash cords) and medicine (as far as the treat-

Like a church

ment of burns), gaining thereby many novel ideas for use later on. In fact, his use of them shows what a good mixer he really was, for Shandy itself requires cool clear courage as well as a certain amount of ginger.*

---

* Readers acquainted with the Cambridge Poets will recognise Sterne's claim to an eminence in verse at least comparable to that which belongs to him in prose:

At Cambridge many years ago, in Jesus was a walnut tree;
The only thing it had to show, the only thing folks went to see.
Being of such a size and mass, and growing in so wise a college,
I wonder how it came to pass it was not called the 'Tree of Knowledge'.

Slimming Treatment Introduced

Unlike Sterne, who was definitely an odd fellow, Addenbrooke of St. Catharine's was a mason, as well as a very clever doctor, and he founded Addenbrooke's to check the fatty degeneration of the dons which was now alarmingly obvious.

Loud-Speaker Installed at King's

Simeon of King's was a saint. He had not intended to be one when he came up, but the Dean said he had to. He therefore set out to convert his bedmaker and her friends to Christian practices, and was so successful that he was at once recognised as a most remarkable man. Later his voice was heard everywhere. That was because the Rector of Yelling trained him.

Higher Mathematical Criticism

Paley, of Christ's, was not a Christian Scientist: he was a Christian Mathematician, and that is much more exciting. It was, in fact, the first time anybody had succeeded in being both, and the field of discovery offered by this application of mathematics to Biblical lore was so rich in good things that many people decided to explore it for themselves. In the end Bishop Colenso, a John's man, showed from his study of the Pentateuch alone that:

(1) The number of boys in every Hebrew family must have averaged 42.

(2) The mother of Moses must have been at least 256 years old when he was born.

(3) On the occasion of the Second Passover, the priests sacrificed 50,000 lambs at the rate of 400 a minute.

(4) The number of warriors assembled in a court that could not hold more than 5,000 at the most generous estimate was 603,350.

But this was much further than Paley intended the application of mathematics to go.

Paley's Mischievous Suggestions

Many dons did not like Paley because they felt he was quietly making fun of them. He once pointed out that as some of the Thirty-Nine Articles contradicted themselves, not even their authors could expect anybody to believe all of them—which the University authorities did. And when Pitt returned to Cambridge as Prime Minister, an occasion on which the dons were naturally thrilled at the thought of the nice presents they would receive, he tactlessly suggested that a suitable text for the University sermon would be: 'There is a lad here which hath five barley loaves and two small fishes; but what are they among so many?'

Wordsworth at Face Value

Although Wordsworth was exceptionally brilliant in after life, at St. John's he was just normally so, being little different from the other students. He admits that he wasted his time at Cambridge:

> For myself
> I grieve not; happy is the gowned youth
> Who only misses what I missed, who falls
> No lower than I fell.

He did not think much of the dons

> —men unscoured, grotesque
> In character, tricked out like aged trees

—or even the unoffending Cam which he
> could have wished
> To see . . . flow with ampler range
> And freer pace.

And he strongly objected to being made to go to chapel:

> Was ever known
> The witless shepherd who persists to drive
> A flock that thirsts not to a pool disliked?

Tricked out like aged trees

But he enjoyed the little mathematics he did, and from his discovery that the three angles of a triangle together make two right-angles derived:

> A pleasure quiet and profound, a sense
> Of permanent and universal sway
> And paramount belief.

So it is clear that he was very much like everybody else and really didn't do any work at all. That is why he had to write about his Cambridge days in blank verse.

Coleridge Upholds the Decencies

Coleridge of Jesus, on the other hand, was always bright. Even when preaching in a Unitarian chapel he wore a sky-blue coat. That was because he was most particular about clothes. A well-conducted world, he said, would be a 'pantisocracy'—one, that is, in which everybody wore proper pants. They would then make fewer bloomers, of course.

Then, too, far from finding pleasure in mathematics, as Wordsworth did, one day he took a party of friends and 'sallied forth to the apothecary's house with a fixed determination to thresh him for having performed so speedy a cure' on his mathematical tutor who had been half-drowned in a duck pond. This explains why he came to be dipped in his own exams.

CHAPTER TWENTY

WHILE these important men were doing their stuff, as the saying was, the University authorities were doing their best to start Downing. This was because Sir George Downing was a bad baronet and had not really intended to found a college at all.

University's Magnanimous Attitude

Sir George's grandfather had also been a very wicked man, so wicked, indeed, that he became 'excessive rich'. Pepys, who knew all about that sort of thing, said outright that he was 'a most perfidious rogue'. So it is not surprising that Sir George was a poor type lacking the right ideas on education. The University authorities, however, did not mind this when the money came to them on the death of his relatives without heir. He was dead too, and as they pointed out, *pecunia ipsa non olet*.

Praiseworthy Foresight of Downing Dons

Although the University hurried to the Court of Chancery and won their suit in only five years, another fifty had to pass before the college was in working order, and it has yet to be finished. But the dons have been very clever. Already they have marked the spot with a cross where the chapel is to be by burying one of the Masters there.

Downing's Inconspicuous Prominence

To make the most of all this money, the Downing authorities decided to have a college bigger and more magnificent than any other, and they would put it where everybody could see it. But although, when objections were raised to Parker's Piece and Castle Hill, they chose a site that was undoubtedly exposed to view at the time, so many shops and houses have since been built round about that nobody can see the college at all. In no other way, however, can Downing be said to be an obscure college.

Oddly enough, Downing is really very old. Being designed in the classical Grecian style, it can be compared only with the Fitzwilliam Museum. Being hidden, too, it escaped the ravages of the Gothic invasion.

The Goths Invade Cambridge

This invasion was very terrible and quite changed the face of Cambridge. Several colleges—among them King's, Sidney, Corpus and Trinity—have never been the same since, and, worst of all, the many pinnacles and turrets left over were simply lumped together to form an entire new range of buildings at St. John's. But the Goths cannot be blamed for the 'unbeautiful object' which rises 156 feet above the surrounding Backs. That is merely the tower of the University's new library.

The University Sees Red

The University authorities offered no serious opposition to the Gothic invasion, but they strongly objected to the proposal to bring the railway to Cambridge. At its best, they said, the station could only be *faux-Gothique*; at its worst, what it is. Also it was 'morally dangerous' for gentlemen *in statu pupillari* to travel that way. All the same, they were unable to stop the trains—a signal failure, of course.

Isolationist Policy of the Dons

But they did not relax their opposition. If they could not prevent the railway from coming to Cambridge, they could

Morally dangerous

still stop the undergraduates from using it, and they not only did so but they also made the company put the station so far from the town that only undergraduates of considerable athletic stamina would ever think of walking so far. And when they heard that the company proposed to bring people *to* Cambridge as well as take them from it, the Vice-Chancellor himself wrote to the directors pointing out that the proposals were 'as distasteful to the University authorities as they must be offensive to Almighty God and to all right-minded Christians'.

Tempora mutantur, non et mutamur in illis, as the dons neatly put it.

Festina Lente

Once the railway had come to Cambridge, the question arose: should the trams be run from the town to the station? It was felt that if the horse were allowed to sit down and rest

If the horse were allowed to sit down and rest

sufficiently often, the scheme would be possible, and in the end the townsmen had their way and showed that it was. But to be on the safe side, intending passengers for the railway took care to catch a tram the day before.

The further suggestion that the trams should be run along the platform itself in order to spare intending passengers that last gruelling half-mile from the booking office to the trains, was turned down by the railway authorities on the grounds that they themselves proposed to run local trains up and down the platform.

Time Marches On

Beyond doubt the University at this period was losing its grip, and quite dreadful things were happening. Elizabeth's statutes, which had done duty for three hundred years, were replaced by ones that opened the door to 'many new and distinct branches of knowledge', and before the century was out, the dons were even allowed to marry—which was a most disturbing innovation because the dons were so keen to take advantage of it that it started not only the 'woman question' but the afternoon tea-party as well, and that was definitely a bad thing.

The 'Woman Question' Explained

It is quite wrong to suppose that because the University does not allow women full membership and a share in

Admire them immensely

control, Cambridge men do not like ordinary women. They admire them immensely, so much indeed that they have named one of the principal thoroughfares in the town —T.P.—in their honour. It is the other sort, the extraordinary women, that they do not like, for only extraordinary women seem to attend lectures and want to run the University. Being bachelors by birth if not by achievement, Cambridge men see no point in being ruled by extraordinary women before their freedom is inevitably terminated by ordinary ones. Therefore they have kept the running of the University in their own hands, holding that woman's place is in the home—*ne famula ultra cubile*, as they say; hence the bedmaker, of course—and looking upon Newnham and Girton with the suspicion that is justifiably drawn to any barracks housing a monstrous regiment of women.

Entrance Examination Introduced

As the students now had to learn so many more difficult subjects, like History and Moral Sciences, some of the dons thought it would be a good idea to make them sit for a preliminary test to show they were capable of doing so. But this required serious thought because for centuries the students had got along splendidly with no examination at all, other than that for the B.A. itself, and fifty years passed before the idea was approved.

The test has now become the entrance examination to the University, and it is known officially as the Previous from the examiners' habit of saying to the unsuccessful candidate: 'Sir, you have been a little previous. Go.' Candidates, however, prefer to call it the 'Little-Go'.

The Common Touch at King's

Then, after four hundred years, the manners of Eton boys having at last improved sufficiently to make a finishing school unnecessary, King's was turned into a proper college, and, as anybody could now go there, it soon became almost normal. But old King's men were deeply shocked when its boat made four bumps in the Mays, and they not only wrote angry letters but they even sent telegrams deploring this intrusion of the athletic spirit.

Bathing Arrangements a Washout

Plumbing, too, was overhauled. The word itself comes from *plumb* meaning 'that which is upright and proper', and by plumbing at Cambridge is meant that appreciation of spiritual and bodily cleanliness for which Cambridge men have always been outstanding. *Mens sana in corpore sano,* as they put it. For that reason washing has always been a serious problem at Cambridge, particularly as there was only one Bath — in Bene't Street — and that was fitted primarily for uvularic lavage. The dons, in fact, did not think anything else was necessary because, as they pointed out, students are in residence for only eight weeks at a stretch, and it was not until the other day, after the students had been forced to go tubbing on the river, that ordinary washplaces were built and the meaning of the old expressions 'having a Bath' and 'going Bathing' extended to cover ordinary washing.

Only eight weeks at a stretch

Students Deprived of Historic Right

Finally the University had to give way even to the Mayor, and now the students would never dream of being rude to him if only because in these days of free education he might win. If he happened to be the Master of a college they would certainly lose.

Jocund Dawn in the Market Place

All this came about by arbitration at the end of the last

century, and the Mayor and Corporation were so astonished at their victory that they presented the arbiter with 'a handsome silver candelabra valued at 300 guineas' for which they had no further use. As Shakespeare said, night's candles were undoubtedly burnt out. But the dons, though magnanimous, were not happy. They saw that this decline in the University's authority was not wholly a good thing, and they were right. Once the proctors had the power to arrest and imprison 'common women, vagabonds and other persons suspected of evil, coming or resorting to the town', and now that they haven't, the town is flooded with such undesirables as income-tax collectors and civil servants generally, as well as retired naval officers and the London School of Economics. As the dons ruefully say, *homini inch das, yard capit.*

CHAPTER TWENTY-ONE

WHILE all these changes were taking place, Cambridge men were not only being as brilliant as ever: they were also becoming so numerous that any record of them must necessarily be a mere catalogue. Melbourne of Trinity, Canning of King's, Palmerston of St. John's, Sedgewick of Trinity, Herschel of St. John's, Tennyson, Thackeray, Byron and Macaulay, all of Trinity, Darwin of Christ's—the list is inexhaustible because it is always being added to. Rupert Brooke of King's, Priestley of King's, His Majesty King George of Peterhouse, Jack Hulbert of Caius, the brothers Ashton of Trinity, Jack Hobbs of Trinity Street. . . . Oxford has nothing comparable.

Oxford Written Off

The extent of Cambridge superiority was clearly shown not long ago when the two universities fielded teams of poets for the annual cricket match at the Elysium Field. The sides on that occasion were:

Cambridge	*Oxford*
Mr. Spenser	Mr. Drayton
Mr. Marlowe	Sir Philip Sidney
Sir John Suckling	Mr. Carew
The Reverend Mr. Herrick	Colonel Lovelace
Mr. Milton	Mr. Collins
Mr. Dryden	Dr. Johnson
Mr. Gray	Mr. Landor
Mr. Wordsworth	Mr. Shelley
Mr. Coleridge	Mr. Matthew Arnold
Lord Byron	Mr. Swinburne
Lord Tennyson	Mr. William Morris

Cambridge won at a canto by several sonnets, of course.

Pastimes of the Great

Byron was particularly naughty while in residence. He kept a tame bear in his rooms and said he was going to run it for a fellowship because it reminded him of the Trinity

Up the garden path

dons—only it was better mannered. Nor was Tennyson altogether nice. He led an innocent lady right up the garden path. And Thackeray was definitely snobbish. Darwin, on the other hand, spent his time beagling.

But most remarkable of all was Oscar Browning, the King's undergraduate. He never grew up although, as a don, he became very donnish indeed.*

Cambridge Pre-Eminence Again Recognised

The period is also remarkable for the coming of the Apostles, a renewal of the divine interest which the University found most gratifying. Sterling of Trinity, a most worthy man—hence, of course, the sterling worth of anything—looked after their welfare and saw that nothing embarrassing occurred as it often does in the Oxford Group Movement. Cambridge, with its high regard for Alma Mater, is aware of the dangers of public confession. That is why, when Oxford proudly says, 'Ah, but we have a Group Movement, we have!' and invites everybody to join as if Oxford alone can lead the world to salvation, Cambridge merely chuckles and declines, saying, *'Non in illis pantaloonibus!'*

Freedom of Speech Emphasised

Being a good man, Sterling also started the Union, the well-known institution on Mill Road. Before it moved there, it met at the 'Red Lion' and was much more convivial than it is now.†

* Readers acquainted with the Cambridge Poets will remember the appeal:

> O.B., oh be obedient
> To Nature's stern decrees;
> For though you be but one O.B.,
> You may be too obese.

† Readers acquainted with the Cambridge Poets will recall the lines:

> The Union Club, of rhetorical fame,
> Was held at the Red Lion Inn,
> And there never was Lion so perfectly tame,
> Or who made such a musical din.

It has proved, however, a debatable project, many speakers arguing that it is too much like a workhouse.

Lofty Aspirations of Cambridge Students

Anybody at a loose end can join the Union, but other clubs demand definite and at times exacting qualifications from their members.   Intending cat-burglars, for example, join the Night Climbers or local Alpine Society and scale such hazards as the Drain-Pipe Chimney in St. John's New Court and the Chetwynd Crack in King's Chapel, or maybe the Sunken Drain-Pipe in the University Old Library and the Trinity Kitchen Plateau.   Then there are nursery climbs for beginners in all colleges.   These, for the most part, are the spiked railings and first-floor windows by which passage through the porter's lodge can be avoided after midnight.

As evidence of their skill, climbers often leave some simple domestic article prominently displayed on the heights. This lends a touch of the incongruous to an otherwise austere skyline, but it should not be taken as indicating that the colleges are in any way jerry-built.

Stern Attitude of College Deans

Students who amuse themselves like this are severely punished if caught because they are supposed to be in their rooms after midnight, not on the tiles.   Nor is it sufficient to enter college just in time to observe the letter of the law. To the student who does that the Dean says sternly: 'I see, Mr. Jones, that on seven nights last week you came in at five minutes to twelve.'   For the rest of the term Mr. Jones therefore comes in through the coal shute or over the railings, and his conduct is blameless in the eyes of the Dean.

Very naughty students are rusticated—sent down, that is, for a period of restful contemplation in the country— but only Rural Deans can inflict this punishment.

Restful contemplation in the country

'Wine is a Mocker'

Rustication was once an excuse for most improper rejoicing. The students would first hold a service of Bacchic character, and then a mock funeral or 'mocker', the wake of which, or procession of irreverent students, appropriately stretched as far as Chesterton. This meant that before the cortege reached the station, traffic in the town was completely disorganised. That is why the University authorities now insist that the corpse departs quietly in a taxi. *Mortui mortuos sepeliant*, as they cleverly say.

Playfulness of Modern Students

Once upon a time the students used to trundle hoops down Petty Cury and play marbles on the Senate House steps, but the University authorities now discourage them, just as they do about lighting fires on Market Hill and being rude to the Mayor.   But they do not always succeed.   Not so very long ago a Trinity man blackened his face and put on a night shirt, and arriving at the station as the Sultan of Zanzibar, received a proper civic welcome, but only the Mayor thought that was rude.   Then some of the students amused the townsmen by opening Tutankhamen's tomb on Market Hill, but, as they explained, they only did it there for the public convenience.

Cambridge Blues

Cambridge men have always been very keen on manly games and sporting things—particularly the Oaks—and those who are exceptionally good and play for the University are coloured blue to show how good they really are.   This is done by standing them about places like Fenners for a short time.   Cambridge blues are thus very famous and important, and quite distinct from ordinary blues such as the Boston, Twentieth Century and Reckitt's. Oxford has nothing like them, of course.

CHAPTER TWENTY-TWO

IN addition to being very brilliant and clever, Cambridge men are remarkable because they never live: they always keep—which shows how well they are preserved.   This is because they are so well looked after in college.

The College Hierarchy

In order of importance to the student, the college authorities are:
    (1) The Head Porter.
    (2) His Gyp and Bedmaker.
    (3) The Butler and the Kitchen Boy.
    (4) The Dean.
    (5) The Chaplain and the Bursar.
    (6) His Tutor.
    (7) The Master.

Mr. Peters at the Gate

The Head Porter is very important indeed. Strangers, seeing him for the first time, mistake him for the Master—unless, of course, they have already run into the Master. Then they are certain. His duty is to see that the students do not stay out too late or go out after 2200 hours, the Cambridge streets then being notoriously dangerous. He therefore makes a point of knowing everybody. And his memory is disturbing. 'Let me see, Mr. Brown,' he will say without hesitation although Mr. Brown has grown a beard since they last met, 'isn't there a little matter of a sedan chair I paid for one night in '68 when you returned from the 'Awks temporarily embarrassed?' As the students cleverly put it, *janitores et elephantes nunquam obliviscuntur.*

Mr. Peters at the gate

Fine by Degrees and Beautifully Less

The word 'gyp' which is applied to the gentleman who looks after the staircase on which the student keeps, derives from *gyps*, the Greek word meaning 'a vulture'. This is because in addition to looking after the staircase, he does for the student. He has a bedmaker to help him, and as all bedmakers are compelled by their union to wear big cloaks under which they carry large baskets, both these officials are very important.*

Very important

The butler and kitchen boy are less so because they are more remote, but the student must always depend to a certain extent on their goodwill for his standard of living, so they obviously rank higher than the Dean. His activities

* Readers acquainted with the Cambridge Poets will recall the pathos of the lines:

> Bedder! Oh, Bedder!
> Bring back my cheddar,
> Bring back my cheddar to me

are, as we have seen, mainly repressive and not really difficult to avoid.

The Chaplain is apt to be a nuisance in his endeavour to fill the college chapel before breakfast, but he is not otherwise important. Nor is the Bursar whose insistence on the payment of college bills concerns parents more than the student, as a rule. And that leaves the Tutor and the Master who are quite unimportant although they cannot be ignored altogether.

Curious Behaviour of Tutors

Tutors like to think of themselves as being *in loco parentis* —which is very odd though not so odd as their method of discharging this duty. Apparently as a cure for the unsatisfactory influences of home life, they have their foster children in their rooms and smoke at them. They are very clever, of course, and also very untidy. Usually they keep everything on the floor—where, indeed, the student will probably find himself when he accepts their invitation to an armchair for the first time. It is not done, however, to comment upon the absence of adequate springs. Armchairs in Cambridge seldom have adequate springs—if any springs at all.

Realistic Attitude of Fitzwilliam House

The Master is naturally extremely old and wise. He probably knows all about the Quantum Theory and the lesser byways of Andorra, but he is quite harmless. Nevertheless there will be dark rumours about him. The unkind will say that he no longer speaks even Latin, finding the grunt sufficient for intercourse at High Table. Also, it is alleged, he makes sibilant noises when taking soup. But it is not necessary to sit near High Table. And if the student can find a reasonable excuse for refusing the breakfast invitation, he will not be bothered at all.

It is, in fact, difficult to understand why a college troubles about having a Master though, in view of the traditional lewd speech of the students, there is something to be said for Fitzwilliam House. They have a Censor.

Extremely old and wise

Inevitable Popularity of Cambridge

Fitzwilliam House is a recent addition to the University which is now very big indeed because all discerning young men want to go there. The difficulty is to find somewhere to put them, and young men who cannot get into a proper college have to form a non-collegiate or improper college by themselves.*

Not long ago, however, a number of good men founded an unusually proper college in memory of Bishop Selwyn who had rowed in the first University Boat Race. But they would allow only young men who were 'willing to live economically' and combine 'sober living and high culture ... with Christian training' to go there. It therefore made only a small impression on the housing problem.

* Readers acquainted with the Cambridge Poets will recall the lines:

> To conclusions let nobody leap.
> The division quite simply denotes
> That penned in a college are sheep,
> While those in the Billy are goats.

Oxford Shortcomings Explained

Cambridge men are naturally very proud of their colleges, but they are even more proud of their University. That is why they are so different from Oxford men. A Cambridge man, when asked, always admits that he is one, quite shamelessly, but an Oxford man will hedge and say he was at Merton or Balliol or some such college of which his questioner has probably never heard. That is because logic is not taught at Oxford, and Oxford men have not therefore learned to argue from the general to the particular.

This fundamental difference between the two Universities is apparent even on the river. At Cambridge men pole

Billy-goat

their punts from the stern so that the punts move forward while they look steadfastly ahead, as is right and proper, but at Oxford men pole from the bows so that their punts always go backwards however much they themselves look into the future. This clearly explains why Oxford never gets anywhere in the Boat Race.

Cambridge Superiority Acknowledged

That Oxford has some good points, Cambridge readily concedes, even to the point of admitting that among the great universities of the world Oxford comes a good though hardly close second. After all, that was the verdict when

Sir Thomas Lipton decided the controversy once and for all by arbitration.

SAUSAGES

Cambridge . . . 1s. 4d.
Oxford . . . 10d.

There is really no more to be said.